BEASTIES

BEASTIES

How to Make 22 Mischievous Monsters That Go Bump in the Night

Diana Schoenbrun

Photography by Tory Williams

A PERIGEE BOOK

A PERIGEE BOOK
Published by the Penguin Group
Penguin Group (USA) Inc.
375 Hudson Street, New York, New York 10014, USA

Penguin Group (Canada), 90 Eglinton Avenue East, Suite 700, Toronto, Ontario M4P 2Y3, Canada (a division of Pearson Penguin Canada Inc.) • Penguin Books Ltd., 80 Strand, London WC2R 0RL, England • Penguin Group Ireland, 25 St. Stephen's Green, Dublin 2, Ireland (a division of Penguin Books Ltd. • Penguin Group (Australia), 250 Camberwell Road, Camberwell, Victoria 3124, Australia (a division of Pearson Australia Group Pty. Ltd.) • Penguin Books India Pvt. Ltd., 11 Community Centre, Panchsheel Park, New Delhi—110 017, India • Penguin Group (NZ), 67 Apollo Drive, Rosedale, North Shore 0632, New Zealand (a division of Pearson New Zealand Ltd.) • Penguin Books (South Africa) (Pty.) Ltd., 24 Sturdee Avenue, Rosebank, Johannesburg 2196, South Africa
Penguin Books Ltd., Registered Offices: 80 Strand, London WC2R 0RL, England

While the author has made every effort to provide accurate telephone numbers and Internet addresses at the time of publication, neither the publisher nor the author assumes any responsibility for errors, or for changes that occur after publication. Further, the publisher does not have any control over and does not assume any responsibility for author or third-party websites or their content.

Copyright © 2010 by Diana Schoenbrun
Photography by Tory Williams
Interior design by Georgia Rucker
Illustrations by Steve Karp

First edition: August 2010

Library of Congress Cataloging-in-Publication Data
Schoenbrun, Diana.
  Beasties: how to make 22 mischievous monsters that go bump in the night/Diana Schoenbrun; photography by Tory Williams.
    p.   cm.
  Includes index.
  ISBN 978-0-399-53597-0
  1. Soft toy making. 2. Bestiaries. 3. Animals, Mythical. I. Title.
  TT174.3.S35 2010   745.592'4—dc22   2009053973

PRINTED IN THE UNITED STATES OF AMERICA

10 9 8 7 6 5 4 3 2 1

Most Perigee books are available at special quantity discounts for bulk purchases for sales promotions, premiums, fund-raising, or educational use. Special books, or book excerpts, can also be created to fit specific needs. For details, write: Special Markets, Penguin Group (USA) Inc., 375 Hudson Street, New York, New York 10014.

Contents

Introduction

Perhaps you're gazing into the night sky viewing a strange dark figure flying above, or you take a peek in the wrong cave and smell smoke, or you find someone's been eating your favorite ice cream. You've probably just encountered a Beastie.

Beasties are mysterious monsters who are hidden away. They are the misfits of the animal kingdom who do not play by the rules. Their magical powers and kooky habits make them outsiders to any ordinary living being. Be on the lookout for these bizarre, hair-raising, and sometimes malevolent creatures. You may be familiar with some of the more dangerous ones, such as the Siren or the Werewolf. But not all Beasties have malicious motives! Some can be helpful, like the Baku, which eats up nightmares so you don't remember them in the morning, or the Tomte, who protects your home and cleans up any leftover messes.

Whether Beasties are real or mythical remains a mystery. Your favorite Beasties might be part animal or human or anything in between, but every Beastie in this book is soft, squeezable, huggable, and lovable.

This is your chance to make a Beastie of your own. Now go, craft, and make lots of monster mischief!

Beginning Your Beastie

Before you make a Beastie, make sure you have everything you'll need. Here is a list of basic supplies to keep in your Beastie toolbox:

- Hand-sewing needles

- Embroidery needles

- Straight pins

- Fabric scissors: *Sharp scissors are important for cutting fabric and felt. Keep a pair of scissors for fabric only, and don't use them on paper because it will dull them.*

- Paper scissors: *Use a set other than your fabric scissors for cutting patterns.*

- Dressmaker's chalk, white-colored pencil, or erasable fabric marking pen: *Use this for tracing patterns onto fabric.*

- Tape measure or ruler

- Pencil

- Stuffing stick, chopstick, or spoon

- Seam ripper: *You can use this tool to pluck out any wrong stitches you may make, without ruining the fabric.*

- Card stock: *You can cut your pattern pieces out of this sturdy paper. An old file folder or the back of a cereal box works, too.*

- Stuffing: *Use a lightweight material to fill the inside of the Beastie.*
- Lint brush or tape: *This is useful to clean off fuzz and excess fibers while sewing.*

Each project will tell you how much fabric, felt, or trim you will need. Save any leftover scraps for later projects and put them into a leftover scrap bag: your Beastie Bag.

Fabric

Your local fabric, craft, and discount stores carry many types of fabric you can use for making Beasties. Or, rather than buying new cloth, consider repurposing fabric that's already in your closet. Older, vintage fabrics can give your Beasties a nostalgic feel, as if they came from the past.

Whatever you decide to use, always make sure your fabrics are clean. Fabrics such as cotton and corduroy can be easily machine washed. Felt, upholstery, and faux fur should not be machine washed. Always check the material's cleaning instructions beforehand. Lint brushes are helpful to remove excess fibers when using different fabrics together; a faux fur, for example, can shed all over cotton.

SPECIAL FABRIC CONSIDERATIONS

The more you work with different fabrics the more you will understand their weight and flexibility. Cotton, corduroy, and lightweight linen and denim are easy fabrics for beginners to start with. Here are a few helpful notes for handling certain fabrics:

Faux Fur. Faux fur, or fake fur, comes in many different styles. The fabric is made of strands, often referred to as "pile," that can vary greatly in length. Some faux furs have straight, crimped, curly, or shaggy pile. Pick faux fur that feels and looks the best to you. Depending on how thick and long the faux fur is you may be able to machine sew or hand sew. I suggest when hand sewing faux fur to use a larger needle and either use a double strand of thread or a sturdier thread such as one marked button, coat, or upholstery thread.

Felt. Felt is a special type of fabric that comes in a rainbow of colors and does not fray, which means you can leave the edges unsewn. Before you buy felt it is good to note the different types. Acrylic felt is the least expensive and the most widely available in craft stores. It is usually sold in 9 x 12 inch sheets. Wool felt is more expensive than acrylic felt, but it's thicker and more durable, and it feels nicer. Depending on the store, you can buy wool felt by the yard or in single sheets. For a felt that's more durable than acrylic and less expensive than wool, acrylic-wool blends are another good option.

Upholstery. Upholstery fabrics are made for furniture coverings so they tend to be thicker than most clothing fabrics. Don't choose one that is unmanageable. I tend to use leftover upholstery scraps that I have collected or find in the sale bin. Sometimes stores will get rid of discontinued sample books or sell them to you at a bargain. These books are great because of the variety of small fabric swatches included.

Trim

Decorations can give your Beastie that extra flair. Feel free to customize your Beastie with pom-poms, ribbon, rickrack, lace, shoelaces, yarn, buttons, beads, googly eyes, feathers, and sequins. Look beyond the typical embellishments and add jewelry, charms, and toy parts. Always keep your eyes open for special bits and pieces to collect and add to your Beastie, and store them in your Beastie Bag. You never know when your Baba Yaga witch may need a new glitzy broach or when your Yeti needs a scarf.

Please note: If you plan to give a Beastie to a young baby or child, keep your Beastie extra soft and entirely made of felt and fabric without any excess trim or any hard trim such as buttons, beads, and pipe cleaners.

Thread and Floss

Sewing thread comes in a variety of colors and can be used for hand sewing or machine sewing. You can purchase polyester thread or polyester-cotton blends.

Upholstery thread, button thread, and coat thread are stronger and useful for sewing thicker, heavier fabrics such as certain wools, faux furs, and upholstery. I usually choose thread that matches or comes close to the color of fabric that I am sewing. For each project I have listed many colors but feel free to experiment and use fewer colors, one color, or contrasting colors that peek through the fabric.

Embroidery floss comes in an array of colors and is usually made of cotton. It's sold in small bundles or skeins with six strands. Each project will instruct you to use either two or three strands at a time. When using floss, it's easiest to cut a long piece to work with that is about 12 to 14 inches long.

Stuffing

Natural and synthetic fiberfill is sold at craft and fabric stores. Both are equally fluffy and light and are good to use in these projects. Polyfill, or polyester fiberfill, is a synthetic fiber. A new fiberfill made of corn is also available; it is a natural fiber and slightly softer than the synthetic kind. I also find that the natural type bunches into balls less when filling your Beastie. Other options for stuffing include old tights and fabric scraps or pellets.

When stuffing your Beastie remember the fiberfill will condense so you will probably use more than you think. One bag will supply you with more than enough for one project. Use small amounts at a time and fill to the corners and crevices of the fabric first. A stuffing stick, chopstick, or spoon can be used to help push the stuffing into place. Continue to fill the Beastie until it is full and even, not lumpy. Beasties can range from squishy to firm. The body should look plump and the fabric should be filled. But don't overfill. You'll know if you've overstuffed if the Beastie's seams are busting out and the fabric is bulging with wrinkles.

Craft Glue

Craft glue is perfect for attaching small bits of felt and decorative trim. The glue dries clear and is safe and nontoxic. I've noted throughout the projects when it's best to use craft glue instead of sewing. (But if you prefer not to use glue you can always hand sew certain trim instead.) Cotton swabs come in handy when applying craft glue. A small amount goes a long way. Apply the glue to the back surface of the felt or trim and press onto the top of the fabric surface. Don't use too much glue or it will spread out onto the fabric. Always read the directions on the glue for more details regarding setting and drying times.

Patterns

Each project includes patterns for the pieces you'll need. Begin by enlarging the pattern on a photocopier to the specified percentage. Next, cut out the pattern pieces, pin the paper pattern to the wrong side of the fabric, and cut around the pattern. An alternative you may prefer is to enlarge the pattern but then trace it onto card stock. This way your pattern pieces will stay flat. Place the card stock on the wrong side of the fabric and trace around it with your fabric chalk or other marking pen or pencil. Then you can cut the fabric along the lines.

You will notice in the "cut from patterns" sections that some projects may instruct you to cut in reverse, which means you simply flip the pattern over. Pattern pieces that are asymmetrical need to be turned over so that you cut a fabric shape for the front and back side. The patterns will also note which fabric to cut and how many cutouts are needed.

In the cases where patterns are not included, the instructions give the dimensions of the shape to cut freehand.

When transferring the patterns you may want to include placement details or you can eyeball them later. The patterns show where eyes, mouths, and noses should go, or you can use the photos as a guide. If you prefer to be more exact, draw lightly with chalk or the erasable fabric pen where you want to place the details.

Please note: The patterns include a ¼-inch seam allowance unless the project notes otherwise. Beasties or parts of Beasties that are hand sewn will not have the seam allowances and you will sew close to the fabric edges.

Sewing Basics

Sewing is the nuts and bolts that keep your Beastie together. The projects will instruct you to sew by hand or machine. All the Beasties in this book can be hand sewn, so if you do not have a sewing machine you can still make them. I suggest hand sewing a backstitch or whipstitch, but feel free to use whatever stitch is most comfortable for you. If you use a whipstitch, you will be sewing along the edges with no seam allowance and your Beastie will end up slightly bigger than the measurements given.

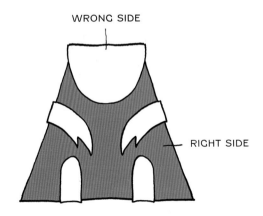

WRONG SIDE

RIGHT SIDE

**SEWING ON THE RIGHT SIDE
VERSUS THE WRONG SIDE**

Throughout the book the instructions will refer to the right side of the fabric versus the wrong side of the fabric. The instructions will explain how to position the fabric and which side you will be sewing on. The right side is the front side—the side meant to be seen. The right side has the pattern, print, fur, raised top, or distinct weave. The wrong side is the back of the fabric that you will not want to see and it will be on the inside of the finished Beastie. Felt is the exception: It does not have a wrong or right side, unless you use embossed felt.

IRONING

Having an iron is helpful if your fabric gets wrinkly. When sewing many parts such as legs, arms, and bodies together, the fabric can wrinkle when turning right side out. A quick press with the iron will keep your Beastie's fabric looking smooth. Just be sure to check your iron's setting so as not to burn your fabric.

MACHINE SEWING

The projects in this book use a simple straight stitch that can be done on your sewing machine. Since no machine—whether new or old—is perfect, I find it helpful to always test the fabric first. Once you load the thread and bobbin, sew on a scrap piece of material to make sure the stitch is taking well and adjust thread, tension, or needle, if necessary. Other machine stitches you may use include these:

Zigzag Stitch. A stitch made by increasing the stitch width on your sewing machine. Adjust the stitch length in combination with the width to get the desired zigzag look (see the Bloody Mary and the Ccoa projects).

Topstiching. A decorative stitch sewn on the right side of the fabric to join two pieces of fabric together. Sew parallel to the edge of the fabric, ⅛ to ¼ inch in. Use a contrasting color if you want the stitches to show well.

Scribble Stitch. In the projects for the Cyclops and Cailleach Bheur I refer to sewing scribble stitches. This can add a subtle decorative look, or if done in a large space it can add more prominent design lines to plain fabric. Use contrasting colors and even try one color of thread in the spool and another in the bobbin of your sewing machine. Sew scribble stitches as if you were scribbling or freehand drawing; the sewing machine needle becomes your pencil. Change directions, make straight lines and curves, and change the stitch length.

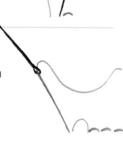

SEWING BY HAND
The projects can be sewn using a variety of simple hand stitches; these may be more functional, such as for attaching fabric together, or decorative, or both.

Backstitch. A strong stitch that mimics the stitches of a sewing machine. Use the backstitch to attach two pieces of fabric together or to embroider decorative details on Beasties. The line of stitches is worked from right to left. (Left to right will be easier if you are left-handed.)

1. Bring your needle from the back side of the fabric through to the front side and reinsert it into the front of the fabric ⅛ inch to the right of where it emerged.

2. Bring the needle back up through the fabric again ⅛ inch to the left of the stitch you just made.

3. Reinsert the needle into the front side next to the previous stitch and continue.

4. Repeat this process (steps 2 and 3) in the direction of your line, keeping the length of the stitches equal.

Blanket Stitch. A visible stitch used to bind edges of fabric together and add decoration. The line of stitches is worked left to right.

1. Bring your needle out along the front side of fabric near the edge of the fabric.

2. Poke needle into fabric at the desired height of your stitch and bring needle through fabric edge with the trailing thread caught by the tip of the needle; pull thread.

3. Continue so stitches are equal length.

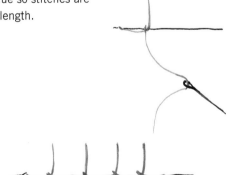

Cross Stitch. A decorative stitch in the shape of an X.

1. Bring needle up through fabric and poke it back down at a diagonal.

2. Bring your needle out through the fabric directly above where your last stitch began, and continue so the next stitch is parallel to the previous stitch.

3. Repeat process.

4. When you reach the end, reverse directions and bring your needle above your last stitch. Repeat, laying parallel stitches over the existing stitches to create an X pattern.

French Knot. A simple decorative knot that is perfect for making small eyes as well as other patterns or designs.

1. Bring the needle up through to the front side of the fabric. Hold the thread tight in your left hand while you wrap the thread around the needle two or three times. You can make bigger knots by twisting the thread around the needle multiple times.

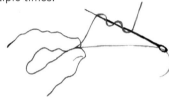

2. Push the needle in next to the hole (do not bring needle through the original hole) and pull the needle through the knot to the back of the fabric.

3. Your finished knot should be tight.

Ladder Stitch. A hidden stitch used to attach fabrics together for limbs and other parts.

1. Sew on top, from one piece of fabric into the next piece so the stitch is perpendicular to the seam.

2. Underneath, bring the needle parallel ⅛ inch along the fabric seam (like a running stitch from underneath) and then back up through the fabric and repeat. When you pull the thread tight the stitches will barely be noticeable.

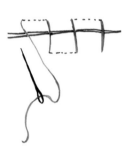

Running Stitch. A basic hand-sewing stitch that attach two pieces of fabric together.

1. Knot the thread and bring the needle into the fabric.

2. Sewing from right to left, bring the needle over, under, over, under. Make the stitches on top of equal length, while the stitches on the back side should be half the length or smaller than the stitches on the top.

Satin Stitch. A decorative stitch sewn to fill in an area—a series of straight stitches close together.

1. Bring a threaded needle through the fabric and then up in a vertical motion and back down into fabric, making a single straight stitch.

2. Come back out through the fabric to the right, next to the first stitch.

3. Repeat to fill the area in.

Whipstitch. A strong overcast angled stitch that joins two edges of fabric together.

1. Moving from right to left, bring the needle through the first piece of fabric and up into the second. Sew going into the second fabric so the stitch is at a slight angle. Then bring the needle back through both pieces of fabric so it is to the left of the original point that you entered.

2. Continue the next stitch parallel to the one before.

Beastie Time

Deciding on which Beastie to make first should not be a treacherous choice.
Each project is marked with a skill level: = **EASY** = **MEDIUM** = **ADVANCED**

Try beginning with an easy project, such as the Tomte, and work your way up to conquering a more challenging one, like the Dragon.

Instructions are provided so you can create your Beastie as shown in the photo. But feel free to customize your Beastie and make changes with fabrics, colors, etc. What would happen if Baba Yaga wore polka dots instead of stripes? Could you make a lady Cyclops without the beard and give her long hair and rosy cheeks?

Most important, have fun!

No Beasties were harmed while making this book.

ADARO

This fish-man swims in the waters of the Western Pacific near the Solomon Islands. Swimmers, divers, surfers beware! Don't be fooled by the sight of a colorful rainbow. The Adaro will slide down after a sea storm and command his flying fish to attack and destroy trespassers.

SKILL LEVEL

FINISHED SIZE: 12 inches wide by 13½ inches high

Materials

FABRIC
- 11 x 23 inch lime green pinwale corduroy
- 4 x 8½ inch shimmery spandex

FELT
- 1 sheet of navy blue
- scrap of white

TRIM
- 2 navy blue beads

THREAD
- white, navy blue, lime green

STUFFING

Preparation

CUT FROM PATTERNS:
- *From corduroy:* 2 body shapes
- *From spandex:* 2 hat shapes (cut 1 in reverse)
- *From navy blue felt:* 4 fin shapes, 1 nose shape, 1 eyebrow, 1 left and 1 right ear
- *From white felt:* 2 eyes

Instructions

1. Pin hat pieces to body pieces so right sides are facing in, and machine sew to attach. Place one body piece, right side facing up, on your work surface. Place one fin piece pointing inward on each arm and leg (X to X). Place other body piece, right side facing down, on top, and pin together, making sure fins stay in place. Machine sew to attach fins to the arms and legs.

2. Next, place left and right ears between the two body layers of fabric pointing inward (Y to Y), and pin together. Sew entire body, leaving stuffing opening unsewn for turning right side out. (When you sew along the arms and legs make sure to fold fins away from the seam so they do not get sewn in.)

3. Turn body right side out. Fill body firmly with stuffing, first filling head, fins, arms, and legs, and then the rest of the body. Sew stuffing opening closed with a small whipstitch.

ADARO

4. For this project, I prefer to sew the face last. Sew eyes to eyebrow with a whipstitch. Next, sew a bead on each eye with four or five stitches to secure. Then sew completed eyes/eyebrow to body.

5. Fold nose in half and sew a whipstitch down the long side. Place the nose on the face and sew small stitches around the base of the nose to attach.

6. Finally, embroider with a double strand of navy blue thread a V-shaped mouth. Sew a backstitch but starting on the top side of the fabric. Leave extra thread loose on both ends of mouth when starting and finishing the backstitch. After sewing the mouth, knot the thread at both ends and trim, leaving ¼ inch of thread hanging.

CUSTOMIZE YOUR BEASTIE

Make a funky rainbow beaded necklace for your Adaro to wear. Or make a flying fish: Draw a simple fish shape. Trace and cut it out from felt and sew on a bead for each eye. Or try using embossed felt. Remember that the embossed side is the right side.

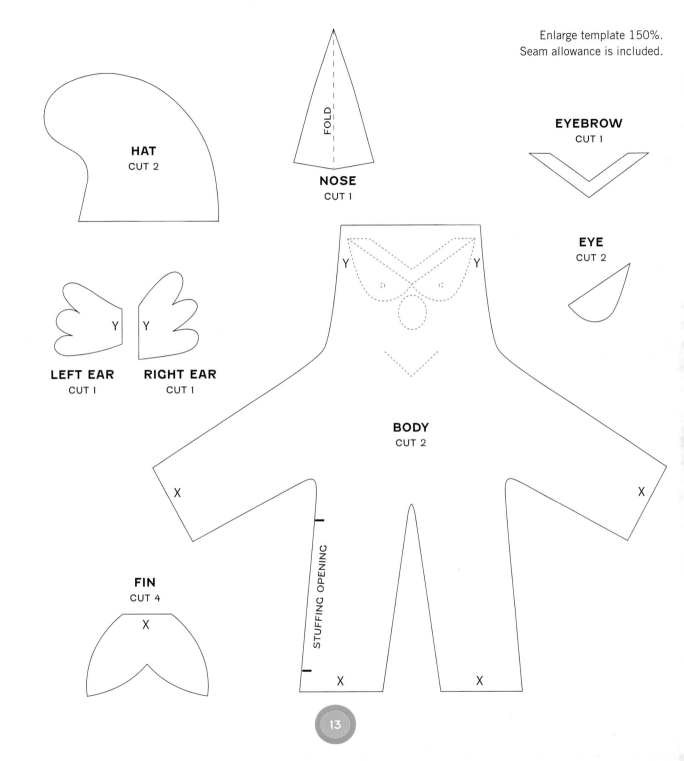

Enlarge template 150%.
Seam allowance is included.

HAT
CUT 2

FOLD

NOSE
CUT 1

EYEBROW
CUT 1

EYE
CUT 2

BODY
CUT 2

LEFT EAR
CUT 1

RIGHT EAR
CUT 1

STUFFING OPENING

FIN
CUT 4

Land ahoy! A floating island in the Mediterranean may appear to be a perfect paradise for a few sailors to come ashore on. However, the Asp Turtle is deceptive. Disturbing him, especially during a slumber, will make him very cranky. He will sink into the sea, bringing everything with him.

SKILL LEVEL

FINISHED SIZE: 11 inches wide by 9¼ inches high

Materials

FABRIC
- 8½ x 24 inch green cotton print
- 6½ x 9 inch green wool or cotton knit

FELT
- 1 sheet of tan
- 1 sheet of green
- scrap of brown

TRIM
- 2 googly eyes
- 3 pom-poms
- 5–7 sequins
- 1 piece of small rickrack 2 inches long

THREAD
- green, tan, brown

STUFFING

NOTE
If your googly eyes are the sew-on type, you can attach with thread. Otherwise you can use a small amount of craft glue.

Preparation

CUT FROM PATTERNS:
- *From cotton:* 2 shell shapes, 4 front leg shapes (cut 2 in reverse), 4 back leg shapes (cut 2 in reverse), 2 tail shapes
- *From wool:* 2 head shapes, 1 island
- *From green felt:* 4 treetops (4 triangles, 2 teardrops, 2 fruit trees), 2 bushes, 3 plants
- *From brown felt:* 8 tree trunks

CUT FREEHAND:
- *From tan felt:* 1 beach (use island pattern as a rough guide but alter the shape and make it slightly smaller in area)
- *From green felt:* 2 eyelids that are half circles large enough to cover the tops of the googly eyes

Instructions

1. Pin together the front leg, back leg, tail, and head pieces so right sides are facing in. Machine sew around, leaving ends open for turning right side out and stuffing. Turn all pieces right side out. Add a small amount of stuffing to fill the front and back legs, head, and tail. They should be filled so they are squishy and not firm. Fill with stuffing to ⅜ inch from opening.

ASP TURTLE

2. Place one shell piece, right side facing up, on the work surface. Pin the front legs, back legs, and tail into position (X to X, Y to Y, and Z to Z), pointing in toward the body. Place other shell piece, right side facing down, on top and pin into position.

3. Machine sew around the shell, except for the side H. Sew carefully so that the legs or tail cannot become loose.

4. Carefully turn shell right side out. First pull the front legs out, then the back legs, then the tail. Fill shell with stuffing so it is full and squishy. Set aside.

5. Place island piece, right side facing up, on top of beach, also facing up. Position the island so the beach felt shows from underneath on certain edges. Machine sew on right side of island, following the edge of green as a guide. Set island/beach aside.

6. Place two tree trunks together and whipstitch sides closed, leaving ⅛ inch unsewn at bottom. Repeat with other pieces to make a total of four tree trunks. Sew edges of treetops (triangles, teardrops, fruit trees) together with a whipstitch and leave a small area open to place tree trunk. Insert end of tree trunk ⅛ inch inside treetop opening and sew closed. Repeat for all trees. Sew sequins onto both sides of the fruit tree. Fold plants in half and sew a whipstitch to close side, leaving ⅛ inch unsewn at one end.

Then sew a pom-pom on top at unsewn end. Cut slits into middle of bushes.

7. Arrange trees, plants, and bushes on island. For each tree trunk, spread apart the bottom, where it was left unsewn, and sew along the base to attach to island. Split the bases of bushes in the same way and sew to island. Sew around bottoms of plants to attach. All trees, plants, and bushes should stick straight up out of the island.

8. Place island/beach piece on top of Asp Turtle shell. Sew a running stitch along the edge to attach to the shell.

9. Attach googly eyes to head. Place eyelids on top of eyes and sew to head. Hand sew rickrack along the seam of the head to form the mouth.

10. Center head in opening (H to H), inserting it to a depth of ¼ inch. Sew a small whipstitch to attach head to shell. Make sure raw edge of cotton is tucked in. Sew closed any remaining side edges.

16

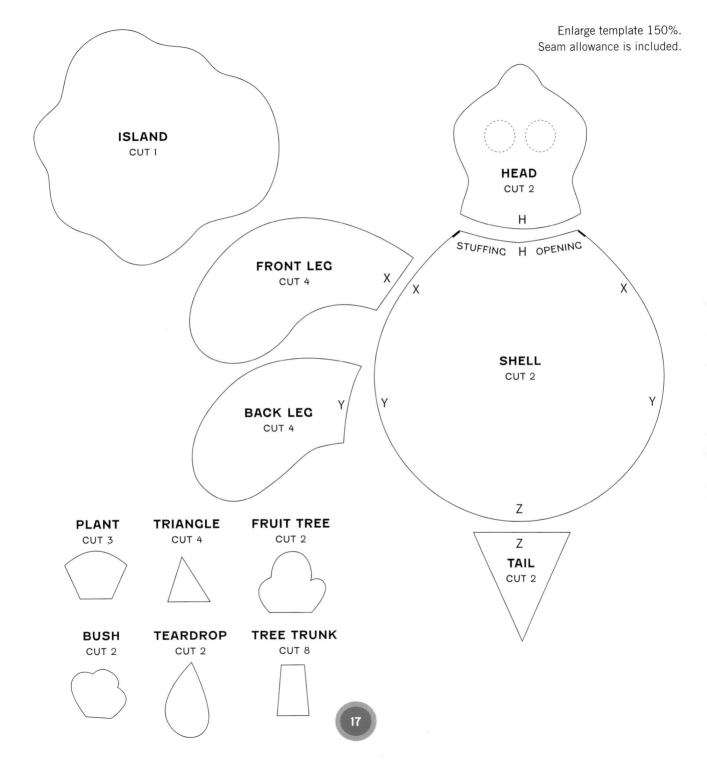

ISLAND
CUT 1

Enlarge template 150%.
Seam allowance is included.

HEAD
CUT 2

H

STUFFING H OPENING

FRONT LEG
CUT 4

X

X

SHELL
CUT 2

X

BACK LEG
CUT 4

Y

Y

Y

Z

PLANT
CUT 3

TRIANGLE
CUT 4

FRUIT TREE
CUT 2

Z

TAIL
CUT 2

BUSH
CUT 2

TEARDROP
CUT 2

TREE TRUNK
CUT 8

If you ever find yourself lost in the tangled forests of Russia and spot a peculiar cabin on chicken legs, be sure to flee. This is the home of Baba Yaga, a craggy witch who is an obsessive cleaner. Her favorite meal is a savory stew of the freshest ingredients she can capture.

SKILL LEVEL

FINISHED SIZE: 5 inches wide by 11¼ inches high

Materials

FABRIC
- ¼ yard cotton poplin pinstripe
- scrap of burlap or loose woven wool knit (optional)

FELT
- 1 sheet of gray
- scrap of black
- scrap of white

TRIM
- black yarn
- green pom-pom
- 2 red beads
- scrap of cotton print (optional)
- 16-inch shoelace or ribbon for apron tie (optional)

FLOSS
- black for mouth

THREAD
- black, gray, white, red

STUFFING

Preparation

CUT FROM PATTERNS:
- *From pinstripe:* 2 hat brim shapes (cut out inside circle section), 2 hat shapes, 2 dress shapes, 4 arm sleeve shapes
- *From gray felt:* 2 head shapes, 2 leg shapes, 2 nose shapes, 2 ears, 4 hand shapes
- *From black felt:* 2 shoe shapes, 1 base (cut full circle), 2 eyelids
- *From white felt:* 2 eyes
- *From burlap:* 1 apron (optional)

CUT FREEHAND:
- *From scrap of cotton print:* 2 small patches for apron (optional)

Instructions

1. Pin hat pieces to top of head pieces, right sides facing in. Machine sew pieces together. Next, pin bottom of head pieces to the top of the dress pieces, right sides facing in, and sew together. Now set aside the two completed triangles (hat/head/dress) that form the body.

2. Fold the bottom edges of the right side of arm sleeves in, and machine sew on wrong side to create finished edges. Pin two arm sleeves together, right sides facing in, and machine sew down both sides, leaving the bottom open for the hand. Turn arm sleeves right side out. Repeat with the other two arm sleeves.

3. Place two hand pieces together and sew a whipstitch to attach. Repeat with other two hand pieces. Insert straight edge of one hand into an arm sleeve about ¼ inch deep. Hand sew a backstitch across to attach hand to arm sleeve. Repeat with the second hand and arm and set aside.

4. Fold felt shoes along dotted line to make a trapezoid. Sew a whipstitch down the side diagonal and other side but leave side L open for legs. Fold legs in half lengthwise and hand sew a whipstitch down the sides. Insert one leg about ¼ inch deep into one shoe opening and hand sew a backstitch across to attach. Sew through top of shoe corner, using a double strand of contrasting thread, and knot a bow to make shoelaces. Repeat with second shoe and leg and set aside.

5. Place both nose pieces together and sew a whipstitch to make the nose two layers thick. Sew on a pom-pom wart. Take one body piece to be used as the front side. Place nose on head and sew a backstitch across top of nose to attach to the head.

6. Sew a bead to the center of each felt eye. Place black eyelids on top and then sew to attach. Sew finished eyes to head. Cut 1-inch yarn strands for eyebrows and sew a few stitches to attach above the eyes. Embroider a zigzag mouth with black floss.

7. Now that the head details are complete, place this body piece on your work surface right side facing up. Place other body piece, right side facing down, on top, and pin together. Machine sew down the sides of the body. Take the base and place legs 1 inch apart and sew small whipstitches to attach the legs along edge of the base. (I find it easiest to sew a few stitches to hold legs in place instead of pinning.) Now pin the base to body, right sides facing in. Make sure shoe/legs are tucked, pointing in toward the body, and aligned on the front side of the body and centered. (Shoelace side should be facing the body.) Either machine sew or hand sew a backstitch to attach base to body. Sewing a circle can be tricky on a machine so sew very slowly. Leave a 2¾ inch opening unsewn to turn right side out.

8. Turn right side out. Fill evenly with stuffing and sew the opening closed with a small whipstitch.

9. Align top of arms to side seams, ⅝ inch above the head/dress seam, and attach with a few small stitches down sides of arm sleeves. Arrange ears on head and whipstitch along side seam to attach.

10. Make two hair pieces with yarn. Cut eight strands of yarn that are 7 inches long and two strands about 5 inches long. Take four strands of 7-inch yarn and use one 5-inch strand to tie a double knot around the middle. Trim off extra. Repeat with the other yarn pieces. Arrange hair pieces where hat meets head on the sides. Sew through the center of the hairpiece knot about four times to attach. Trim hair as you like.

11. Pin hat brim pieces together, right sides facing in. Carefully and slowly machine sew along the outer circumference. Turn right side out and sew around inner circumference. Pull hat brim over and down the hat point until it meets the hat/head seam. The brim should fit snugly and does not need to be sewn.

12. If you are making an apron, fold straight edge of apron down. Machine sew across on the wrong side. Then pull shoelace or a knotted end of ribbon into the apron seam space and out the other end. Hand sew square patches onto apron. The unsewn edges of the apron will fray and give a ragged look. Tie the apron around Baba Yaga's waist and knot at the back.

21

CUSTOMIZE
YOUR BEASTIE
Instead of using pinstripe cotton for the hat and dress, try using old wool suit material that is lightweight. Or add more pom-pom warts to make Baba Yaga even more hideous!

BABA YAGA

Enlarge template 160%.
Seam allowance is included.

HEAD
CUT 2

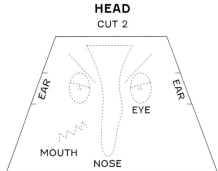

EAR

EAR

EYE

MOUTH

NOSE

HAT
CUT 2

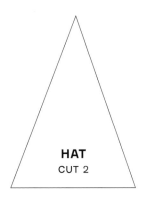

ARM SLEEVE
CUT 4

FOLD

DRESS
CUT 2

STUFFING
OPENING

FOLD

APRON
CUT 1

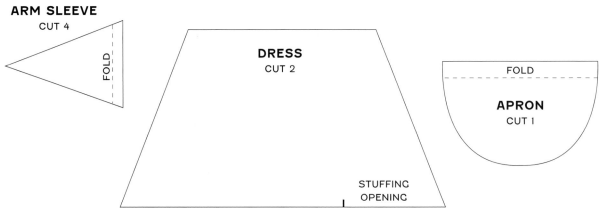

NOSE
CUT 2

HAND
CUT 4

LEG
CUT 2

SHOE
CUT 2

L

HAT BRIM AND BASE
CUT 2

EAR
CUT 2

EYE
CUT 2

EYELID
CUT 2

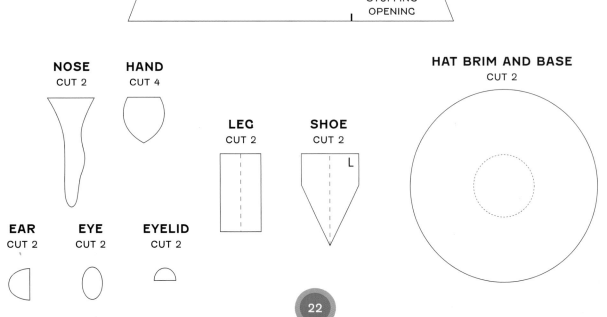

22

Welcome this friendly Japanese monster called Baku, who devours nightmares so you don't remember them. His powerful trunk sucks up the gobbledygook that makes bad dreams and leaves you in a peaceful slumber.

SKILL LEVEL

FINISHED SIZE: 12 inches wide (not including tail) by 7½ inches high

Materials

FABRIC
- 7 x 18 inch cotton spotted print
- 8 x 13 inch gray fleece
- 4 x 6 inch orange cotton knit

FELT
- 1 sheet of orange
- scrap of white

TRIM
- 2 blue beads

THREAD
- white, orange, gray

STUFFING

Preparation

CUT FROM PATTERNS:
- *From cotton spotted print:* 2 body shapes (cut 1 in reverse), 1 trunk top
- *From fleece:* 2 ear shapes (cut 1 in reverse), 2 head shapes (cut 1 in reverse)
- *From cotton knit:* 2 ear shapes (cut 1 in reverse)
- *From orange felt:* 2 eyelids
- *From white felt:* 2 eyes

CUT FREEHAND:
- *From orange felt:* 2 rectangles ¾ x 2¾ inches, 1 rectangle 1 x 8 inches
- *From fleece:* 3 rectangles ¾ x 1½ inches

Instructions

1. Pin a fleece ear to a cotton knit ear, right sides facing in. Machine sew ears together, leaving straight side open. Turn right sides facing out. Do not stuff. Tuck raw edges in so they do not show and sew ears closed with a small whipstitch. Repeat for the other ear and set aside.

23

2. Sew the tail: Align the three gray fleece rectangles on top of each other and sew a whipstitch at one end so all the pieces are attached. Place the sewn edge of the gray fleece rectangles so that ⅜ inch is inserted between the two smaller orange felt rectangles along one of their short sides. Sew a running stitch across to attach. Pin felt together and machine sew a topstitch down each long side of the orange rectangle. Cut gray fleece into fringe for tail hair and set tail aside.

3. Next, align and pin head pieces to body pieces so right sides are facing in. Machine sew to attach.

4. Place one body/head piece, right side facing up, on your work surface. Place tail at back of body as marked on pattern, pointing in toward the body. Place other body piece on top, right side facing down, and pin together. Begin machine sewing at point A below tail. Sew carefully up and over tail, continuing around the body, stopping at trunk opening point B. Leave side B–C open.

Begin at other side of trunk at point C and continue sewing the body (carefully sewing around the curves of feet) and stopping at point D.

5. Turn finished body/head right side out. Fill with stuffing. Begin filling stuffing in small areas of feet and then legs, so they are full and firm, but not too tight.

Continue to fill head and then body. Sew opening A–D closed with a small whipstitch.

6. Now fill trunk with stuffing to the top through the trunk opening (B–C). Cover the opening with the trunk top right side facing out and sew with a whipstitch around to attach.

7. Align ears as shown on pattern and sew with a ladder stitch to attach to head.

8. Sew beads to centers of white eyes and hand sew eyes to head. Next, place eyelids on top and sew to attach.

9. Take the long strip of orange felt for the mane and align at point E. The strip should wrap around the neckline and overlap the head. Sew a whipstitch along the edge of felt along the seam to attach to the neck. Then cut at ¼ inch intervals to make the mane frayed. Be careful not to cut all the way to where the mane meets the neck. Trim lengths of strips as you like. Push mane downward like a collar so stitches become hidden.

BODY   NECK
E

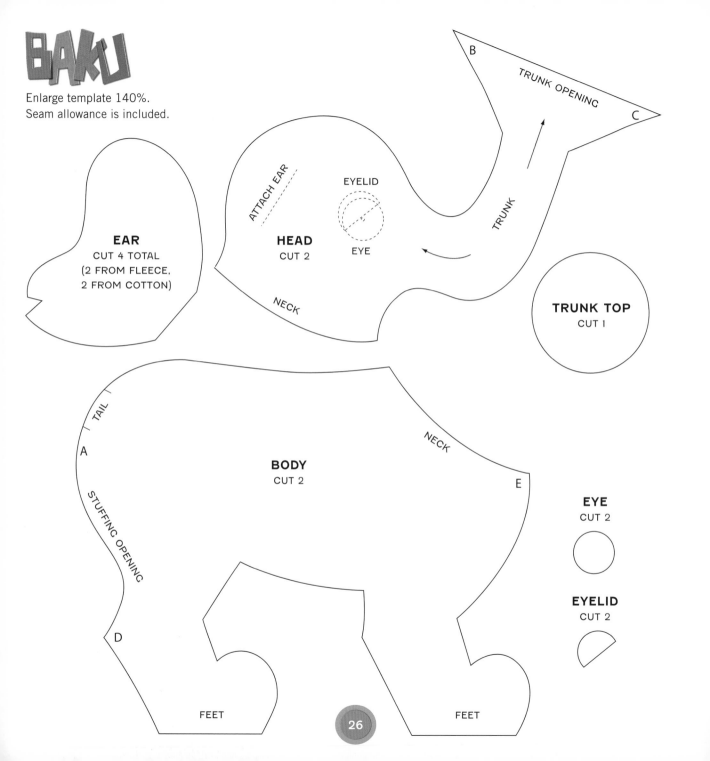

BAKU

Enlarge template 140%.
Seam allowance is included.

EAR
CUT 4 TOTAL
(2 FROM FLEECE,
2 FROM COTTON)

HEAD
CUT 2

ATTACH EAR

EYELID

EYE

NECK

B

TRUNK OPENING

C

TRUNK

TRUNK TOP
CUT 1

TAIL

A

BODY
CUT 2

STUFFING OPENING

NECK

E

D

FEET

FEET

EYE
CUT 2

EYELID
CUT 2

BLOODY MARY

Are you brave enough to summon the spirit of Bloody Mary? Chant her name thirteen times in a candlelit bathroom, and she will leap through the mirror. If you're an acceptable victim she will drag you in. Some say she was a vain queen who went mad while others say she has always been cruel. However, most agree that with her crown of blades and daggers she is certainly scary.

SKILL LEVEL

FINISHED SIZE: 5½ inches wide by 8½ inches high

Materials

FABRIC
- 5½ x 9 inch black velvet
- 3½ x 5½ inch khaki cotton

FELT
- 1 sheet of dark gray
- scrap of red

TRIM
- 3 pearlized buttons
- 11½ inches gathered mesh lace

FLOSS
- black

THREAD
- red, black

STUFFING

CRAFT GLUE

Preparation

CUT FROM PATTERNS:
- *From velvet:* 2 body shapes
- *From cotton:* 2 head shapes
- *From gray felt:* 2 crown shapes, 2 arms
- *From red felt:* 5 droplets

BEASTIE TIP Make an offering of jewelry and Bloody Mary may predict your future. However, misfortune will befall you if she is displeased with your gift.

Instructions

1. Sew a red zigzag stitch about ¼ inch wide down the center of one body piece for the front side.

2. Sew a French knot on two of the red droplets with embroidery floss. Place a small amount of glue on the back of the droplets and adhere to one head piece and allow to set. Embroider a ⅜-inch-wide stitch with three strands of floss to make a mouth. This will be the front head piece.

3. Pin head pieces to body pieces, right sides facing in, and machine sew to attach.

4. Place front head/body piece, right side facing up, on your work surface. Pin arms into position to body (X to X), pointing in toward the body. Then place back body piece on top, right side facing down, and pin. Sew around the head/body, leaving area open for turning right side out and stuffing.

5. Turn head/body right side out. Sew three pearlized buttons on the front of the body.

6. Begin filling small amounts of stuffing first into the head and then into the body until full. Sew the opening closed with a small whipstitch.

7. Cut twenty strands of embroidery floss 6 inches long. Make a hair piece by taking four strands at a time and tying a knot at the center. Make five hair pieces in total. Space hair pieces evenly along the head seam. Sew two stitches through each knot to attach.

8. Align crown pieces together and sew a whipstitch down each side. Sew a droplet on the left, center, and right points of the crown.

9. Align the crown on the head and sew three stitches at the left and right corners to attach to the head.

10. Sew the lace collar by beginning at the center of the back along the body/head seam. Wrap lace three times around. Sew four stitches through lace into back side of the body to secure in place.

BLOODY MARY

Enlarge template 120%.
Seam allowance is included.

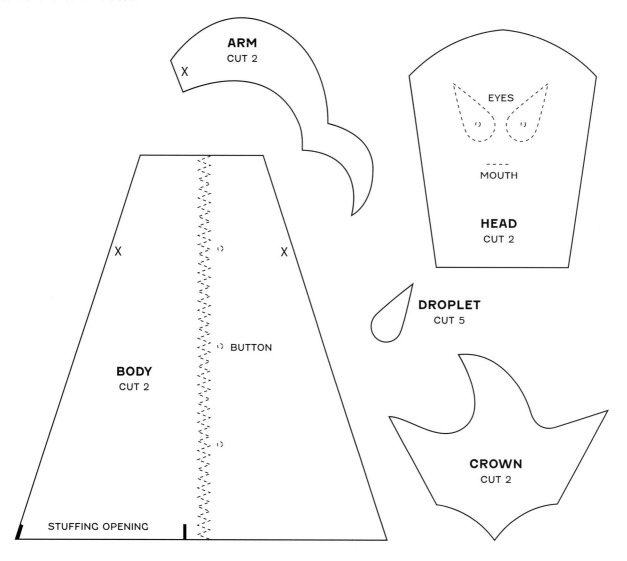

ARM
CUT 2

X

HEAD
CUT 2

EYES

MOUTH

BODY
CUT 2

BUTTON

STUFFING OPENING

X   X

DROPLET
CUT 5

CROWN
CUT 2

CAILLEACH BHEUR

Stay away from this cold lady or risk frostbite. Cailleach Bheur is the blue hag who brings forth winter in Scotland. She roams the land, beating her staff on the ground, freezing the earth, and causing snowfall. The mountains were said to have been formed when stones she collected fell out of her pockets.

SKILL LEVEL

FINISHED SIZE: 5½ inches wide by 11¾ inches high

Materials

FABRIC
- 6¾ x 13 inch dark blue cotton
- 8½ x 20 inch silver shantung *(Note: shantung may be expensive if it is made of silk; a cheaper synthetic version of shantung or other silver fabric can also be used)*
- scrap of shimmery blue

FELT
- scrap of white

TRIM
- 1 bead for the eye
- tiny scrap of rust-colored fabric for tooth

FLOSS
- white

THREAD
- dark blue, light gray

STUFFING

Preparation

CUT FROM PATTERNS:
- *From cotton:* 2 rectangles 6½ x 6¾ inches for head
- *From shantung:* 2 body shapes, 1 base shape
- *From shimmery blue:* 2 pockets (1 full pocket, cut 1 pocket in reverse with a hole cut out)
- *From white felt:* 2 arms, 1 eye

CUT FREEHAND:
- *From rust-colored fabric:* 1 small tooth
- *From floss:* 32 strands 6 inches long for hair

Instructions

1. Place one body piece to be used as the front side, right side facing up, on your work surface. Align pockets and hand sew along the curve from A to B with a wide whipstitch, alternating with a few crisscross stitches. Leave the straight edge along the top of pockets open.

2. Place arms on front piece pointing in toward the body and pin. Then place other body piece, right side facing down, on top and pin. Begin by machine sewing from bottom all the way around, leaving the entire bottom open.

3. Next, pin base to bottom of the body opening with right sides facing in. Machine sewing a circle can be tricky so sew slowly along the circular curve. Leave opening for turning right side out and stuffing.

4. Turn fabric right side out and fill body with stuffing. Sew a small whipstitch to close opening and set body aside.

5. Trace the head pattern on the wrong side of the fabric on only one of the cotton rectangles. Then pin both rectangles together, right sides facing in. Machine sew, following the line you traced. Leave area open for turning right side out and for stuffing. Trim excess fabric around head, keeping scissors ¼ inch away from the stitch line.

6. Turn right side out. Fill head evenly with stuffing, making sure to fill the bumps. (I prefer to stuff the head first because the type of fabric I used stretched and I did not want my embroidery stitches pulled.) Set head aside.

7. Use the sewing machine to sew scribble stitches on the eyeball. You can also draw lines with a fabric marker on felt as an alternative. Sew bead onto the center of the eye and place on head. Sew around eye to attach.

8. Create the other eye by sewing with two strands of floss. Sew a 1-inch backstitch but begin on top of the fabric instead of from underneath. Leave 1 inch of floss hanging loose when beginning the stitch and finishing the stitch. Knot the thread close to the fabric and trim to leave a shorter strand hanging loose. Next, hand sew a zigzag backstitch on top over your horizontal stitch. Again leave extra thread hanging at the beginning and end of stitch.

9. Make a mouth. Hand sew a backstitch with two strands of floss as shown on pattern. Then sew a small stitch to attach the bottom of the tooth along the mouth.

10. Make hair pieces. Tie four strands of floss together with a knot in the center. Repeat so you have eight hair pieces. Sew through the knot with two stitches to attach each hair piece to each head bump along the seam.

11. Sew body to head 1¼ inches up from bottom of the back side of the head. Sew another two stitches directly underneath the bottom of the head to the body at point X.

CAILLEACH BHEUR

Enlarge template 150%.
Seam allowance is included.

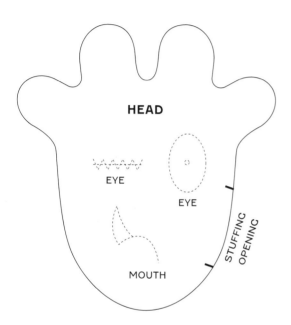

HEAD

EYE

EYE

MOUTH

STUFFING OPENING

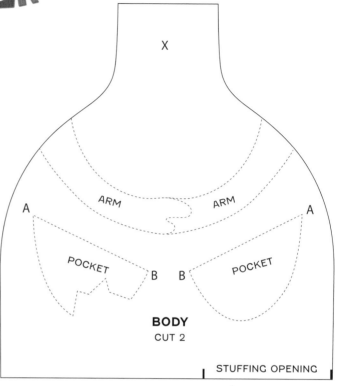

X

ARM

ARM

A

A

POCKET

B B

POCKET

BODY
CUT 2

STUFFING OPENING

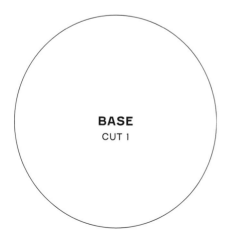

BASE
CUT 1

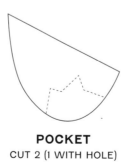

POCKET
CUT 2 (1 WITH HOLE)

EYE
CUT 1

ARM
CUT 2

CCOA

The mountain cat of Peru is no nice kitty. Watch out for the hail the Ccoa spews from his fire eyes and the lightning storms he causes, which ruin crops. Possible havoc can be avoided if the right offerings are made.

SKILL LEVEL 👾👾

FINISHED SIZE: 5 inches wide by 8½ inches high

Materials

FABRIC
- 7 x 18 inch gray-and-black-striped cotton
- 5 x 11 inch iridescent gray fabric

FELT
- scrap of yellow
- scrap of black

TRIM
- 11-inch strand of black yarn
- 2 red pom-poms

THREAD
- black, red

STUFFING

CRAFT GLUE

Preparation

CUT FROM PATTERNS:
- *From striped cotton:* 2 ears, 4 leg shapes (stripes should run in vertical direction), 2 body shapes (stripes should run in horizontal direction)
- *From iridescent gray fabric:* 2 head shapes, 1 tail shape
- *From yellow felt:* 5 teeth, 4 claws, 1 nose
- *From black felt:* 2 eye pupils

BEASTIE TIP Try leaving a bowl of warm milk with honey for the Ccoa to appease it for a while.

Instructions

1. Place one body shape, right side up, on your work surface. Align one head piece, right side up, on top of body as marked on pattern. Machine sew a zigzag stitch from point A to point B to attach head to body. (Practice zigzag stitch on scrap material first to make sure you like the width and size of the stitch. If you do not have a sewing machine, use a crisscross stitch to replace the zigzag stitch.) Sew the zigzag stitch so the head and body fabric lie centered. Attach the other head piece to the other body piece to make the back side in the same manner.

2. Place claws (X to X) on top of the right side of leg so straight edges align and pin. Machine sew to attach claws to legs.

3. Place both head/body pieces, right side facing up, on your work surface. Pin in place two legs, right side facing up, on each body as marked on pattern. Now sew a red zigzag stitch from point C up and around the curve and down to point D on all the legs.

4. Fold tail in half lengthwise so right sides are facing in. Machine sew from point E to F and F to G. Leave end open for turning right side out. Turn right side out and set tail aside.

5. Fold ears in half so right sides are facing in and sew along the long side of the triangle. Leave bottom open and turn right side out.

6. Place one body/head piece, right side facing up, on the work surface. Place ears and tail pointing in toward the body and pin. Then place other body/head piece, right side facing down, on top and pin pieces together. Machine sew the body/head pieces together, leaving area open for turning right side out and stuffing.

7. Turn fabric right side out and fill evenly with stuffing. Sew a small whipstitch to close the opening.

8. Put a small amount of craft glue on the back of each tooth to attach teeth to the head. Allow a few minutes for glue to set. Cut yarn into three strands to make whiskers. The strands can be uneven in length. Bundle the three pieces and tie a knot in the center of the yarn. Place yarn knot in the area where the nose will be, and sew three stitches through knot to attach to head. Then use glue on back to attach nose on top of whiskers and attach to head. You may need to hold nose in place for one or two minutes until glue begins to set.

9. Glue black pupils on pom-poms. Place pom-poms on the top of the head. Sew thread through the back of one pom-pom and then into the seam and out. Sew three stitches to attach pom-pom eye and repeat with the other pom-pom eye.

CUSTOMIZE YOUR BEASTIE
Try using shoelaces, ribbon, or old cassette tape for whiskers. Give your Ccoa a different expression, such as a grinning, frowning, or surprised mouth.

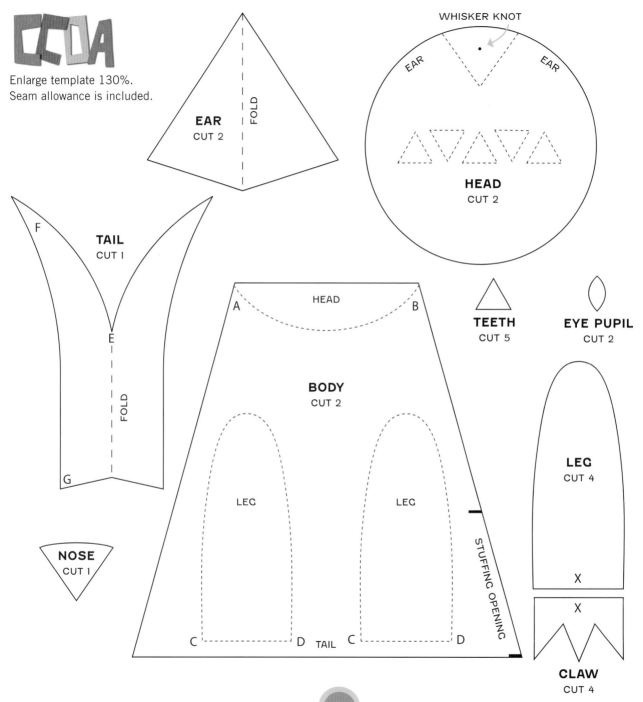

Enlarge template 130%.
Seam allowance is included.

EAR
CUT 2

FOLD

WHISKER KNOT

EAR

EAR

HEAD
CUT 2

TAIL
CUT 1

F

E

FOLD

G

TEETH
CUT 5

EYE PUPIL
CUT 2

A   HEAD   B

BODY
CUT 2

LEG

LEG

STUFFING OPENING

LEG
CUT 4

X

X

NOSE
CUT 1

C   D   TAIL   C   D

CLAW
CUT 4

Beware of the Chonchon bite! If you have a tickle in your throat or are just an old, wrinkly curmudgeon, you may be perfect prey for the bloodsucking Chonchon of Chile. Look and you may see a head flying, flapping its ears through the night air.

SKILL LEVEL 👾👾

FINISHED SIZE: 14 ½ inches wide by 7 ½ inches high

Materials

FABRIC
- 8½ x 21 inch short faux fur or fleece (something fuzzy)
- 7 x 13 inch teal blue wool or cotton
- 6 x 11 inch contrasting upholstery remnant or cotton print
- scrap of brown faux fur

FELT
- scrap of white
- scrap of black
- scrap of red

TRIM
- 2 white beads

FLOSS
black

THREAD
- pale pink, white, teal, red

STUFFING

BEASTIE TIP Close your windows or he will try to fly in for a taste.

Preparation

CUT FROM PATTERNS:
- *From short faux fur:* 1 nose, 2 full ear shapes (cut 1 in reverse), 2 ears with inner ear cut out (cut 1 in reverse)
- *From wool:* 2 head shapes
- *From upholstery:* 2 ear accents (cut 1 in reverse), 1 base

CUT FREEHAND:
- *From white felt:* 2 triangle fangs, 2 circles the size of a dime
- *From black felt:* 2 circles of felt slightly smaller than the white circles
- *From red felt:* 3 drops
- *From brown faux fur:* 6 patches ½–1 inch across

Instructions

1. Place both ears with inner ears cut out, facing right side down, on your work surface. Place ear accents, right side facing down, on top. The ear accents should overlap the edges. Pin fabric layers together. Flip ears over so right sides are now facing up. Sew a small whipstitch around each ear edge to ear accent to attach. Leave ear hair opening unsewn.

2. For each ear, once again flip ear over so right side is facing down. Sew faux fur scrap to back and guide faux fur out through ear hair opening. Flip ear over so finished front ear is right side up on your work surface. Place back ear piece, right side facing down, on top and pin together. Machine sew pieces together, leaving edge A–B open for turning right side out.

3. Turn ears right side out. Leave ears open at edge A–B and set aside. Do not stuff ears.

4. Place one head piece, right side facing up, on your work surface. Pin nose, right side facing up, in place and hand sew around to attach to the head.

5. Place black felt circles on top of white felt circles for eyes. Sew beads to felt circles, sewing through both layers about five times to secure each bead. Arrange eyes on head and sew around white circle to attach to head. Black circle will not be sewn down.

6. Next, sew a mouth using three strands of embroidery floss. Arrange fangs along mouth and sew a small stitch at the bottom of each triangle to attach to mouth. Place red drops and remaining brown faux fur patches on head and sew around each to attach.

7. Place front and back head pieces, right sides up, on your work surface. Use tailor's chalk to draw a zigzag line as shown on pattern on both pieces. Machine sew, following the line. Cut below the stitches, within $\frac{1}{8}$ inch of them, to remove excess fabric. The fabric will fray.

8. Pin heads together so right sides are facing in. Machine sew around head, leaving bottom edge C–D unsewn.

9. Turn head right sides facing out. Pin base piece, right side facing out, along opening C–D and sew a whipstitch to attach to head, leaving a 2-inch opening for stuffing. Fill head with stuffing and then sew opening closed with a whipstitch.

10. Pin together edges of ears (A–B to A–B). Use a ladder stitch or a whipstitch and sew all the way around the front and back side of ears to attach to the head.

CUSTOMIZE YOUR BEASTIE

Give your Chonchon a personalized hairdo. Use extra faux fur, yarn, or feathers to style a full mane, mohawk, or feathery hairdo. Or make multicolored Chonchons and hang them flying from your ceiling!

CHONCHON

Enlarge template 150%.
Seam allowance is included.

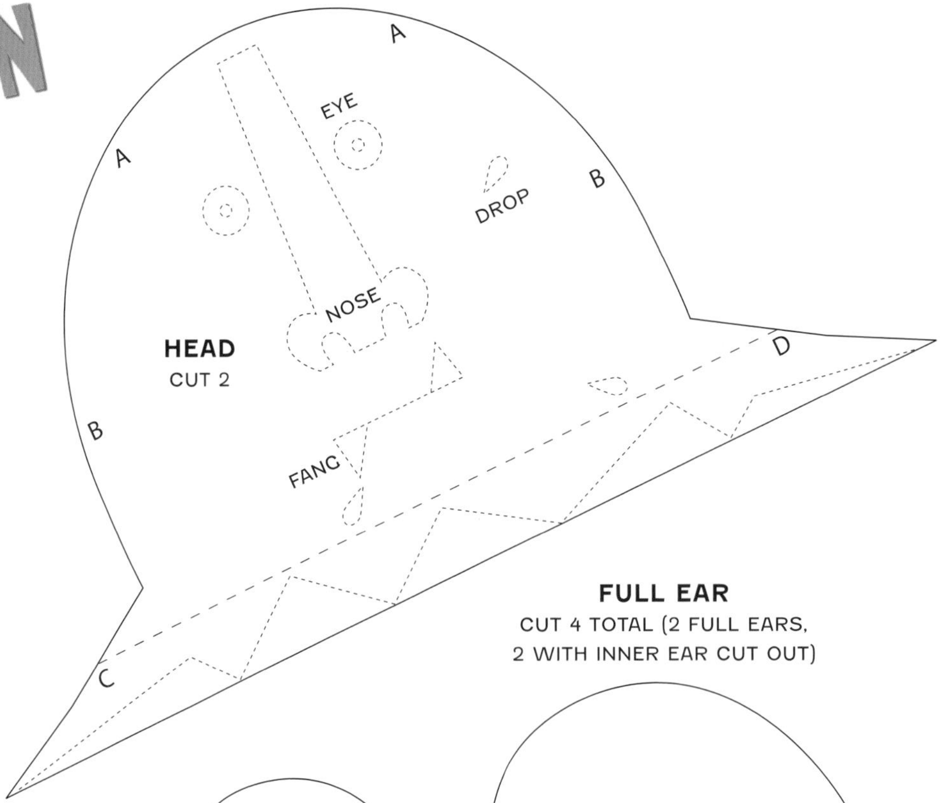

NOSE
CUT 1

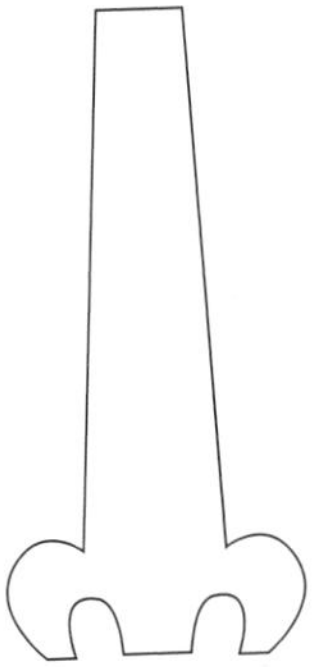

HEAD
CUT 2

A

A

EYE

DROP

B

NOSE

B

FANG

C

D

FULL EAR
CUT 4 TOTAL (2 FULL EARS,
2 WITH INNER EAR CUT OUT)

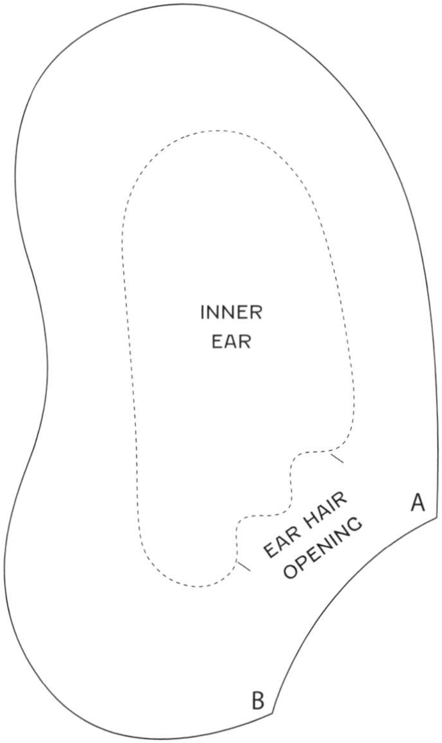

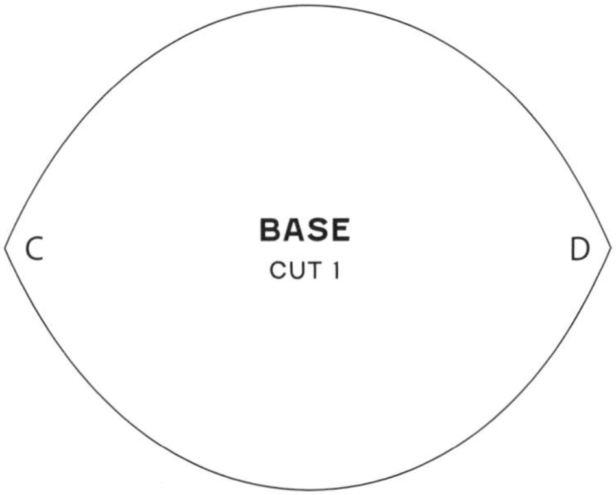

BASE
CUT 1

C

D

EAR ACCENT
CUT 2

INNER
EAR

EAR HAIR
OPENING

A

B

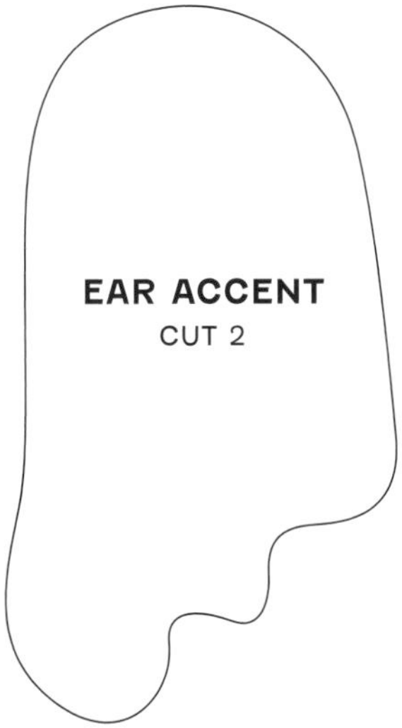

CINNAMOLOGUS

This protector of cinnamon perches high up in the treetops. The Cinnamologus knows how desirable the spice is so she is always on the watch.

SKILL LEVEL

FINISHED SIZE: 8 inches wide (from beak to end) by 4¾ inches high

Materials

FABRIC
- 7½ x 12 inch cinnamon red velvet
- 4 x 4 inch cotton print

FELT
- 1 sheet of yellow

TRIM
- 2 yellow buttons
- 2 pipe cleaners for legs
- blended-color yarn for hair

FLOSS
- cinnamon red, yellow

THREAD
- cinnamon red

STUFFING

Preparation

CUT FROM PATTERNS:
- *From velvet:* 2 body shapes (cut 1 in reverse), 2 wing shapes (cut 1 in reverse)
- *From cotton print:* 2 wing shapes (cut 1 in reverse)
- *From yellow felt:* 2 beak shapes

BEASTIE TIP Try distracting the bird by sprinkling nutmeg—which blinds it temporarily. Then snatch a handful of cinnamon and be gone. Move too slowly and you may be a new spicy bird snack.

Instructions

1. Begin by sewing both beak pieces together with a blanket stitch using cinnamon red floss. Sew down one diagonal and bottom side only. The other side B will be sewn into the body.

2. Next, form the tail: Cut a piece of yarn 26 inches long and fold it in half three times. Cut another piece of yarn 2 inches long and wrap it around one folded end and double knot. Cut the opposite end's loops loose so eight strands hang from the knot.

3. Place one body piece right side facing up on your work surface. Place beak on top (B to B), pointing in toward the body and place other body piece on top, right side facing down. Machine sew from X to Y, over the beak. Be careful when sewing over the four layers of fabric.

Pause at corner Y. Align tail in left corner, at T, making sure all yarn is pointing in toward the body. Knot should lie outside fabric area so it is clear of the seam. Sew from corner Y to Z (down the diagonal), making sure beak is also clear of seam. Next, sew along bottom, leaving opening for stuffing and turning right side out. Turn body right side out.

4. Align and pin wings, right sides facing in. Each wing should have a velvet side (front) and a cotton print side (back). Machine sew along diagonal and one side, and halfway on third side. Turn right side out and use a small whipstitch to close the opening. Do not stuff the wings. Align wings to body (W to W), as marked on pattern. Sew with a small ladder stitch from underneath the wing (cotton print side) to attach to the body.

5. Sew button eyes in place. Cut two 4-inch strands of yarn. Loop one around each button and knot it.

6. Next, make the legs:

a. Measure a pipe cleaner to 11 inches and trim off any extra with scissors. Be careful of sharp wire ends.

b. Measure at 2 inches and fold.

c. Continue to make 1-inch folds until you have three Vs (a zigzag line) and the rest of the pipe cleaner pointing up. Bend pipe cleaner so both straight ends stick upward and are parallel to each other. Push Vs together and extend shorter straight piece over longer straight piece.

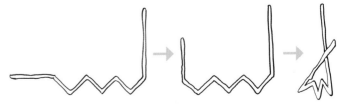

d. Twist each of the three toes together, leaving a tiny space open at the ends for floss.

e. Next, fold long side of pipe cleaner down to meet the end of the twisted part and twist again. Leave a tiny space open for the floss at the top.

f. Using a large needle, pull one end of floss through top of leg and knot. Wrap and twist floss down pipe cleaner toe.

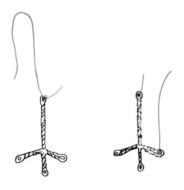

g. Bring floss through loop end and wrap back up each toe and leg until they are covered as shown.

7. Align legs beneath the wing at L. Sew through top loop of leg three times and knot. After legs are attached, fill body with stuffing and close the opening with a whipstitch.

CUSTOMIZE YOUR BEASTIE

You can save time by using yellow pipe cleaners instead of brown. You will not need yellow floss so you can skip steps f and g. Or try using a decorative cotton print instead of the velvet and add feathers to the tail, head, and wings.

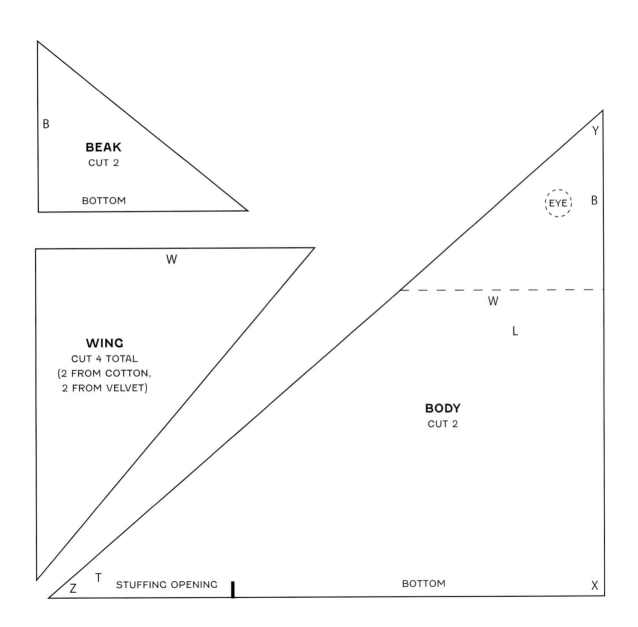

BEAK
CUT 2

B

BOTTOM

Y

(EYE) B

W

WING
CUT 4 TOTAL
(2 FROM COTTON,
2 FROM VELVET)

W

L

BODY
CUT 2

Z T STUFFING OPENING BOTTOM X

Don't cross this one-eyed giant if he wakes up on the wrong side of the olive grove. At one time the Cyclops made thunderbolts, helmets, tridents—you name it. But now he likes to take it easy, relaxing on the hillsides of Sicily, sipping grape juice, and tending to his sheep.

SKILL LEVEL 👾 👾 👾

FINISHED SIZE: 6½ inches wide by about 15 inches high (depending on the length of the faux fur on the head)

Materials

FABRIC
- 14 x 19 inch tan cotton or wool knit
- 2 x 3½ inch piece of faux fur

FELT
- 2 sheets of white
- scrap of turquoise
- scrap of black

TRIM
- 1 small white bead
- 1 large button

FLOSS
- blue

THREAD
- tan, white, blue, a color that contrasts with blue

STUFFING

Preparation

CUT FROM PATTERNS:
- *From knit:* 2 body shapes, 2 head shapes (cut 1 in reverse), 1 eyelid
- *From white felt:* 1 eye A, 2 gown shapes (cut 1 with shorter strap)
- *From turquoise felt:* 1 eye B, 1 mouth
- *From black felt:* 1 eye C
- *From faux fur:* 1 hair piece (set aside the leftover strip for the beard)

CUT FREEHAND:
- *From turquoise felt:* 16 small pieces about ¼ x ¼ inch square for nails
- *From leftover faux fur:* cut a 1-inch-long piece for cheeks and a 2½-inch-long piece for chin beard

BEASTIE TIP To escape the gaze of the Cyclops, hide beneath the bellies of his grazing sheep.

Instructions

1. Pin body pieces together, right sides facing in. Begin by machine sewing at A and continue down and around arms and legs until you reach B. Leave area A–B open for turning right side out and stuffing.

2. Turn body right side out. Fill hands and feet first, then arms, legs, and body with stuffing. Fill arms and legs with small amounts at a time since the inside is narrow. A knit fabric will stretch, so do not overstuff or you will begin to see the stuffing showing through the knit. Close opening A–B with a ladder stitch or small whipstitch.

3. Arrange felt nails on hands and feet. Place four nails per hand or foot. Sew a double stitch through the center of each nail to attach. Set body aside.

4. Take one head piece to use for the front. Begin by embroidering, on the right side, a swirl on both ears and chin using a backstitch with two strands of floss.

5. Center eye B onto eye A. Machine sew with white or contrasting color a scribble stitch on eye B but do not go outside area. Then place eye C on top of eye B in center and sew a scribble stitch again. Hand sew white bead in the center of eye C. Place finished eye on head and sew around eye to attach. Fold straight edge of eyelid under and sew a running stitch across. Place eyelid on top of eye and sew along curved edge to attach. Place mouth on head and hand sew to attach.

6. Place finished head piece, right side facing up, on your work surface. Place remaining head piece, right side facing down, on top and machine sew together. Leave area C–D open for turning right side out and stuffing.

7. Turn head right side out and fill with stuffing. Using a whipstitch, sew hair piece along front and back of head, from C to D. Sew side openings closed.

8. Use faux fur strips for beard. Sew with a whipstitch along left cheek (X to X) and sew remaining fur to chin (Y to Y).

9. Place head between shoulders so head is between A–B as shown on pattern. Attach head to body by sewing a ladder stitch from A to B at back of head. Sew another two hidden stitches underneath the chin at Y so the head does not flop.

10. Pin gown pieces together. Machine sew down sides and turn inside out. Step the Cyclops into the gown and pull up. The longer strap should be in front so it overlaps the back strap. Place large button on top of the back strap and sew through layers of felt to attach straps.

CUSTOMIZE YOUR BEASTIE

Make a crazier-looking Cyclops. Try different color combinations such as violet body fabric and red hair or orange body fabric with blue hair. Or make a friend for the Cyclops: Cut longer faux fur for head hair and get rid of the beard to make a female Cyclops.

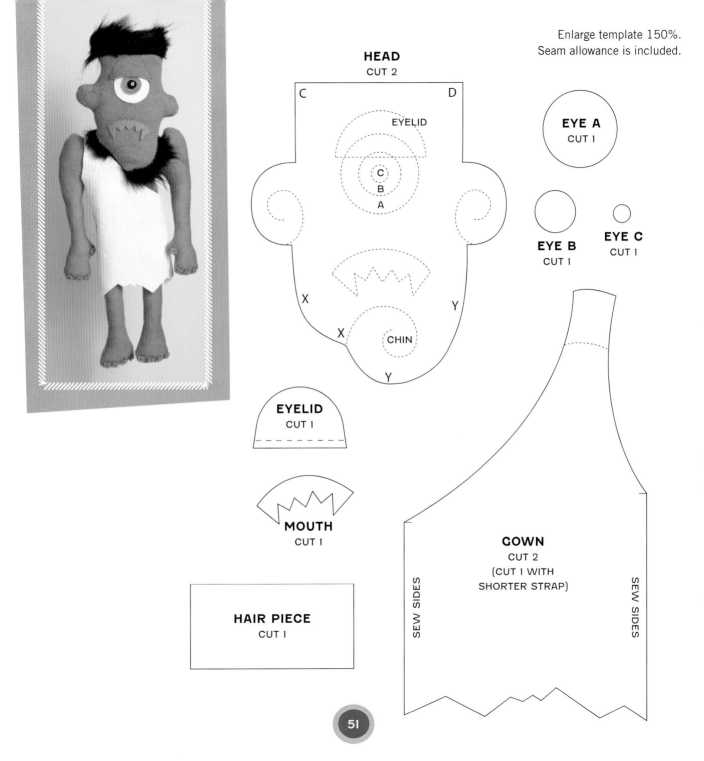

Enlarge template 150%.
Seam allowance is included.

HEAD
CUT 2

C   D

EYELID

C
B
A

X   Y

X

CHIN

Y

EYE A
CUT 1

EYE B
CUT 1

EYE C
CUT 1

EYELID
CUT 1

MOUTH
CUT 1

GOWN
CUT 2
(CUT 1 WITH
SHORTER STRAP)

SEW SIDES

SEW SIDES

HAIR PIECE
CUT 1

Enlarge template 150%.
Seam allowance is included.

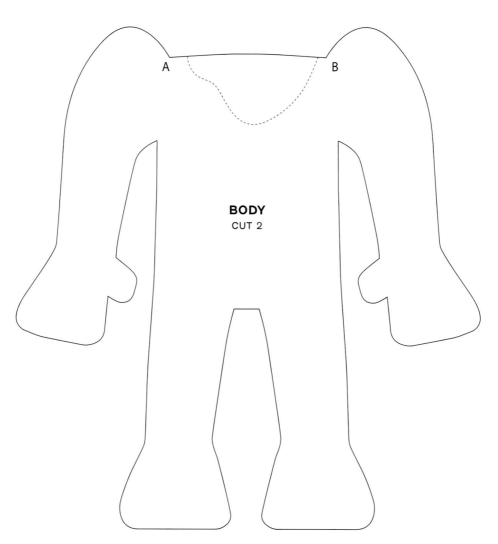

A   B

BODY
CUT 2

DRAGON

This gargantuan flying reptile will make you run for the hills when you experience his flame-spitting, smoky breath. Some try to slay Dragons because they contain medicinal powers, while others try to steal Dragons' treasures.

SKILL LEVEL 🐛🐛🐛

FINISHED SIZE: 11 inches wide by 11½ inches high

Materials

FABRIC
- 18 x 24 inch iridescent dark green fabric
- 5½ x 5½ inch shiny silver-green fabric

FELT
- 1 sheet of lime green
- scrap of red

TRIM
- 2 red sequins

THREAD
- lime green, dark green, red

STUFFING

Preparation

CUT FROM PATTERNS:
- *From dark green fabric:* 2 body shapes (cut 1 in reverse), 2 tail shapes (cut 1 in reverse), 8 leg shapes (cut 4 in reverse), 2 head shapes (cut 1 in reverse), 1 mouth shape
- *From silver-green fabric:* 2 wing shapes (cut 1 in reverse)
- *From lime green felt:* 2 wing shapes, 2 mouth shapes, 2 eyes, 4 front claws, 4 back claws, 10 fangs
- *From red felt:* 2 horns, 1 nostril, 1 tongue

BEASTIE TIP If you are cornered by a fuming Dragon, try dousing his head with water to put out his flame before you become barbecued.

Instructions

1. Begin by sewing the wings. First machine sew with red thread on felt wings the curved lines as marked on the pattern. Pin felt wings to right side of silver-green wings. Make sure there is one left and one right wing that will have lime green facing on the outside with a shiny side on the inside. Machine sew wing pieces together. Leave opening F–G unsewn for turning right side out.

2. Turn wings right side out. Do not stuff. Tuck frayed ends in and sew a whipstitch to close opening. Set wings aside.

3. Next, make the four legs: Place four leg pieces (two left, two right), right sides facing up, on your work surface. Place front and back claws on feet so pointed ends are facing inward. Place other leg pieces on top so right sides are facing down and pin. Sew leg pieces together, leaving an area unsewn to turn right side out and stuff.

4. Turn legs right side out. Fill legs with stuffing so they are firm. Sew opening closed with a small whipstitch. Set legs aside.

5. Pin a tail piece to a body piece (A to A and B to B) so right sides are facing in, and machine sew to attach. Next, pin a head piece to a neck piece (C to C and D to D) so right sides are facing in, and machine sew to attach. Repeat with the other tail, body, and head piece. Place one completed head/body/tail, right side facing up, on work surface and place the other one, right side facing down, on top and pin together. Begin sewing at point A and sew toward the tail and around the body. Leave an opening at the belly unsewn for stuffing. Continue sewing to point D and leave mouth area D–E unsewn. Start again at point E and sew until point A.

6. Place one felt mouth on head (aligning D–E to D–E) and sew around to attach.

7. Turn Dragon's entire head/body/tail right side out through the belly opening. Do this carefully so as not to rip or pull any parts.

8. Fill tail first with small amounts of stuffing until evenly full. You may need a stuffing stick to help. Continue by filling the head and then the body. Use small whipstitches to close belly opening.

9. Sew six teeth, evenly spaced, along the top mouth seam.

10. Next, pin remaining felt mouth to the right side of the iridescent mouth. Sew these pieces together, leaving 1 inch unsewn. Turn right side out, but do not stuff. Sew opening closed with small whipstitches. Place straight edge of tongue at back of mouth near D (felt side) and stitch in place. Sew four teeth evenly apart along the bottom mouth seam. Then attach bottom mouth, iridescent side facing down, to head, using a few stitches at point D.

11. Sew nostril along seam so it wraps around front of head at E. Align horns with eyes (X–Y to X–Y dashed line) and sew along to attach. Sew a sequin in the center of each eye. Then place eyes on head and sew along top to attach to head.

12. Align wings on body (F–G to F–G) with felt sides facing out. Sew with a ladder stitch to attach each along either side of seam.

13. Match legs to body (Z to Z) and attach with a ladder stitch, sewing from the inside of the leg into the body fabric.

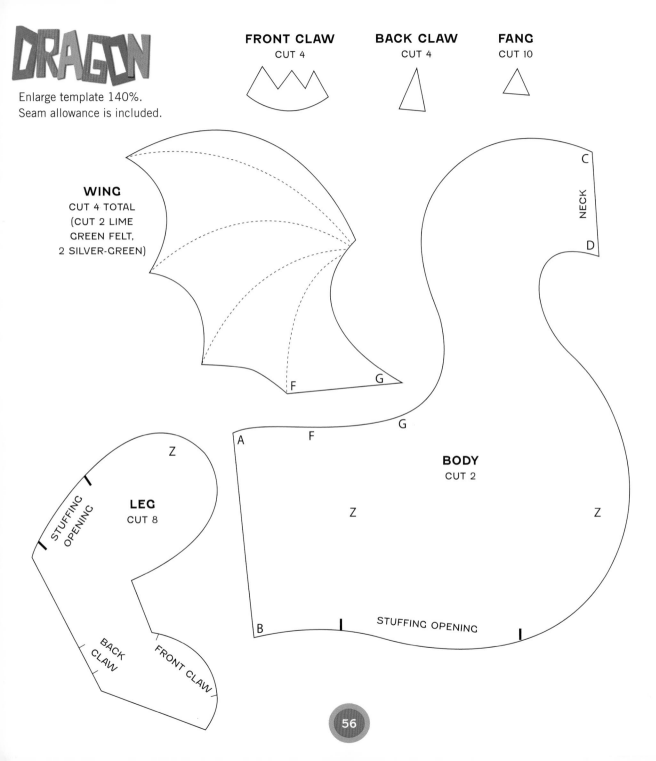

DRAGON

Enlarge template 140%.
Seam allowance is included.

FRONT CLAW
CUT 4

BACK CLAW
CUT 4

FANG
CUT 10

WING
CUT 4 TOTAL
(CUT 2 LIME
GREEN FELT,
2 SILVER-GREEN)

NECK

C

D

F   G

A   F   G

BODY
CUT 2

Z   Z

Z

LEG
CUT 8

Z

STUFFING OPENING

B   STUFFING OPENING

BACK
CLAW

FRONT CLAW

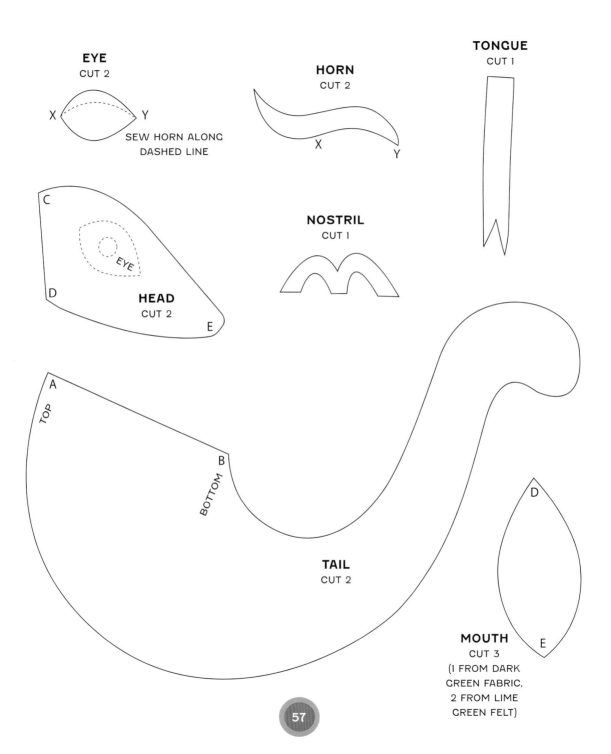

EYE
CUT 2

X · · · · Y

SEW HORN ALONG
DASHED LINE

HORN
CUT 2

X   Y

TONGUE
CUT 1

C

EYE

D

HEAD
CUT 2

E

NOSTRIL
CUT 1

A

TOP

B

BOTTOM

TAIL
CUT 2

D

E

MOUTH
CUT 3
(1 FROM DARK
GREEN FABRIC,
2 FROM LIME
GREEN FELT)

Deep in the lush jungles of Zaire is the creature named Eloko, who guards the fragrant fruits and plants that grow there. Listen for the bells he rings: *ding, ding, ding!*

SKILL LEVEL

FINISHED SIZE: 6½ inches wide by 6 inches high

Materials

FABRIC
- 5 x 10½ inch brown cotton

FELT
- 1 sheet of mint green
- scraps of other green colors
- scrap of white
- scrap of pink

TRIM
- 3 small bells

FLOSS
- navy blue or black

THREAD
- brown or green, white, navy, red

STUFFING

Preparation

CUT FROM PATTERNS:
- *From cotton:* 2 body shapes
- *From mint green felt:* 3 grass pieces A, 2 grass pieces B
- *From other green felts:* 10 leaves, 2 hands, 2 feet
- *From white felt:* 2 eyes, 4 teeth
- *From pink felt:* 2 trunk shapes, 1 snout

BEASTIE TIP Wear earmuffs to block out the sound of the dwarf's magical jingling bells because they can put a spell on you. Otherwise you may find yourself offering him your arm or leg as an hors d'oeuvre.

Instructions

1. With floss, sew about eight satin stitches on center of each eye (they can be slightly uneven in length) and then sew one across in the opposite direction. Choose one body piece to be the front, and place eyes on it and sew to attach.

2. Place both body pieces, right sides facing up, on your work surface. Place one grass piece B on top of each and pin. Machine sew straight across top to attach.

3. Next, place one grass piece A on top of one body piece. The bottom edge of grass A will overlap B. Position hands (X to X) and feet (Y to Y), pointing in toward the body. Now place other body piece on top, right side facing down. Machine sew around the body, leaving area between the feet open for turning right side out and stuffing.

4. Carefully turn body right side out. Cut the sewed-on piece of grass A into strands approximately ¼ inch wide. This will allow the fabric to become less taut and the felt to stick up. Next, align the remaining two pieces of grass A on front and back side and sew a whipstitch along the top to attach. Then cut all the uncut A and B grass layers into strands and trim as you like.

5. Embroider two small circles for nostrils on the snout with a double strand of red thread. Place teeth along trunk (T to T), so teeth are pointing into the trunk. Place other trunk piece on top and sew a whipstitch along the sides. Place snout, with embroidery side facing in, along the straight side opening and sew to attach. Turn right side out. Add a pinch of stuffing to fill the trunk.

6. Place completed trunk onto body and sew to attach curved edge of trunk to body.

7. Place leaves, evenly spaced apart, on both sides of the body. Hand sew at the top of each leaf's point, two stitches on the left and two on the right.

8. Fill body with stuffing. Sew opening closed with a small whipstitch.

9. Cut a 4-inch strand of floss and knot one end. Sew floss into seam at top of body and back out, then thread bell and knot. Sew back into seam and out again, repeating to thread all three bells.

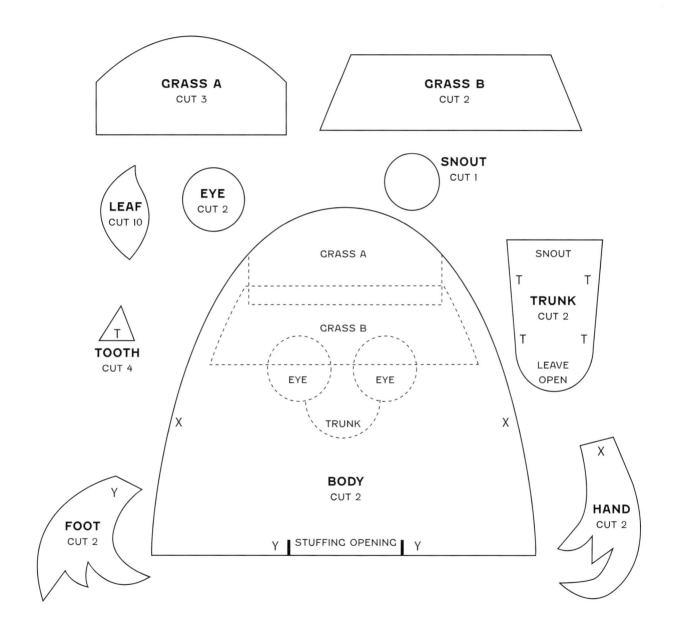

GRASS A
CUT 3

GRASS B
CUT 2

SNOUT
CUT 1

LEAF
CUT 10

EYE
CUT 2

SNOUT

T   T

TRUNK
CUT 2

T   T

LEAVE
OPEN

TOOTH
CUT 4

T

GRASS A

GRASS B

EYE   EYE

TRUNK

X   X

BODY
CUT 2

X

HAND
CUT 2

Y

FOOT
CUT 2

Y   STUFFING OPENING   Y

These tiny flying spirits are invisible to most people. However, you can sometimes hear them singing or feel them flicker through the air. If you leave a cup of fresh berries out for them, they will grant you a wish. Pick too many of their flowers and you will become their foe.

SKILL LEVEL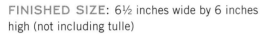

FINISHED SIZE: 6½ inches wide by 6 inches high (not including tulle)

Materials

FABRIC
- 4½ x 10½ inch colorful cotton print
- 7¾ x 12 inch shimmery or plain-colored fabric

FELT
- scrap of white
- scrap of yellow

TRIM
- 2 beads for eyes
- 6-inch square of tulle for hair
- 14-inch ribbon for belt (optional)

THREAD
- colors to match fabrics, a color for the mouth that contrasts

STUFFING

Preparation

CUT FROM PATTERNS:
- *From cotton print:* 2 body shapes
- *From shimmery fabric:* 2 wings
- *From white felt:* 2 heads, 2 feet, 2 ears
- *From yellow felt:* 1 teardrop-shaped nose

BEASTIE TIP Fairies hate the smell of a barbecue. To attract them, plan a picnic instead.

Instructions

1. Pin head pieces to body pieces, right sides facing in. For each, make sure the head piece is centered between points A and B on the body fabric. Machine sew to attach.

2. Choose one head/body piece to be the front side of the Fairy and place, right side up, on your work surface. Hand sew beaded eyes to the head. Sew two stitches at the top of the nose to attach to the head. Use a double strand of contrasting thread to embroider the mouth. Pin the feet into position (X to X), pointing in toward the body.

FAIRY

3. Pin the two head/body pieces together, right sides facing in. Machine sew around the body. Leave the head area A–B unsewn for turning right side out and stuffing.

4. Turn head/body right side out and fill body section with stuffing. Sew a small whipstitch to close head, stopping halfway, at the top of the head.

5. Take the square of tulle and pinch from center to bunch. Hold the bunched tulle and tie a knot around it with thread about ½ inch from tip. Insert knotted end into the head opening about ¼ inch deep. Continue sewing the head seam with whipstitch through the tulle. Add a small amount of stuffing to fill the head and then finish sewing the head closed. Place ears at sides of head and sew to attach.

6. Pin wing pieces right sides facing in. Machine sew around wings and leave an opening unsewn for turning right side out and stuffing.

7. Turn wings right side out and fill with stuffing. Sew a small whipstitch to close the wings.

8. Sew three stitches from the back of Fairy's body into the center of the wings to attach.

9. If you want to make a ribbon belt for your Fairy, cut a 4-inch piece off the ribbon, loop it, and form a double knot at one end. Place loop knot at center of wing and sew through, into wing. Secure with a few stitches. Take remaining ribbon and pull it through the loop like a belt. Tie ribbon around the waist of the Fairy so belt is fitted, and double knot it.

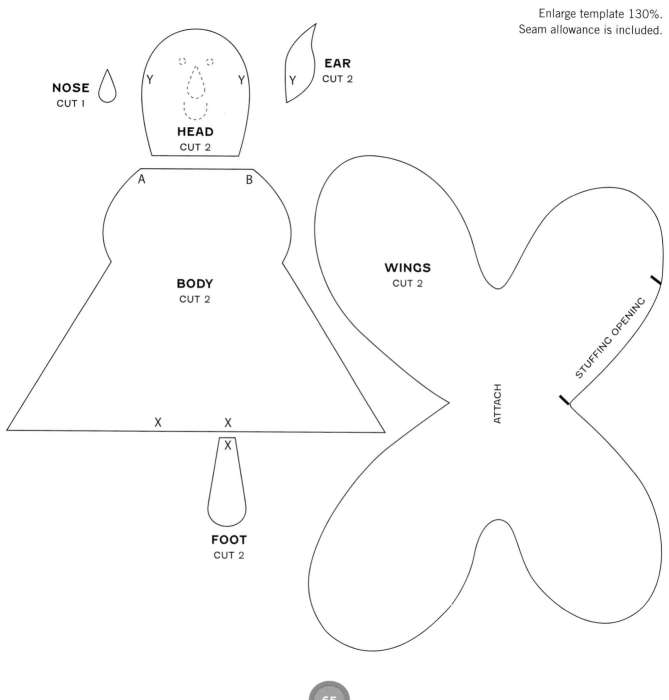

Enlarge template 130%.
Seam allowance is included.

NOSE
CUT 1

Y   Y

HEAD
CUT 2

Y

EAR
CUT 2

A   B

BODY
CUT 2

WINGS
CUT 2

X   X

X

FOOT
CUT 2

ATTACH

STUFFING OPENING

FISH-HEAD ALIEN

This creature is often spotted in the muggy swamps of Brazil. He came to Earth because he wanted to seek out the interesting fish that live in the Amazon. He became friends with the fish and protects them by scaring away fishermen. Those who survive encounters with the Fish-Head Alien tell horrifying stories of his pulsating antennae, which he pokes people with.

SKILL LEVEL

FINISHED SIZE: 12½ inches wide by 10 inches high (not including antennae)

Materials

FABRIC
- 10 x 26 inches blue terry cloth (note: terry cloth tends to stretch a little)
- 9½ x 11 inches bright yellow rayon or cotton
- 7 x 10 inch pink cotton*
- scrap of silver fabric or paper*

FELT
- scrap of white
- scrap of magenta
- scrap of black

TRIM
- 1 sequin
- 7 inches silver ribbon

THREAD
- blue, magenta, yellow

STUFFING

CRAFT GLUE*

Preparation

CUT FROM PATTERNS:
- *From terry cloth:* 2 rectangles 10 x 13 inches
- *From yellow cotton or rayon:* 2 head shapes (cut 1 in reverse)
- *From pink cotton:* 2 T-shirt shapes*
- *From silver fabric or paper:* 1 planet shape*
- *From white felt:* 2 eyes A, 2 teeth
- *From magenta felt:* 1 mouth, 2 eyes B
- *From black felt:* 2 eyes C, 1 shape D*

*Note: Materials and pieces marked with an asterisk are required only if you want to give this Beastie a T-shirt.

BEASTIE TIP The Fish-Head Alien enjoys hearing an intriguing story. If it's a good tale, you will be released.

FISH-HEAD ALIEN

Instructions

1. On the wrong side of one rectangle of terry cloth, center the body pattern and trace it with chalk. Pin rectangle pieces together so right sides are facing in. Machine sew along the body pattern line and leave the top unsewn for an opening to turn right side out. Cut around the body, at least ¼ inch away from the stitching, to remove excess fabric. When cutting around claw make a small slit to separate claws, being careful not to cut any stitches.

2. Turn body pieces right side out. Make sure each arm and its claw are turned all the way out. Begin filling claws by using small amounts of stuffing at a time. Fill the crevices in the claws and then continue to fill the rest of the arms and body with stuffing. The body should be filled evenly and full, but not too firm. Fill body with stuffing to the top of opening.

3. Choose one head piece to use for the front side. Begin by embroidering on the right side of fabric a nose and mouth with a double strand of blue thread. For each eye, hand sew eye A to eye B, and then B to C. Place completed eyes on head and sew around to attach. Sew teeth to felt mouth and then felt mouth to head. Sew the sequin eye to the head.

4. Pin head pieces together, right sides facing in. Machine sew around, leaving an area open for turning right side out and stuffing.

5. Turn head right side out. Fill with stuffing and use small whipstitches to sew the opening closed.

6. Loop ribbon and sew a few stitches to hold loop in place. Then sew ends of ribbon with a few stitches to attach to the head.

7. If you are making the T-shirt, put craft glue on back of silver planet shape and place centered on front right side of T-shirt piece and allow glue to set. Then adhere shape D on top of planet shape with glue. Fold sleeves as marked on pattern into the wrong side. Machine sew on wrong side to make a seam. Then pin together T-shirt pieces, right sides facing in, and sew along sides and sleeves, leaving neck, arm holes, and bottom open and unsewn. Turn T-shirt right side out. Carefully pull arms through armholes of the T-shirt.

8. Place body opening centered against completed head. Body opening should be flush to the bottom of head. Sew a tight ladder stitch all the way around bottom of head to body to attach. I find it works best to sew into terry cloth ⅜ inch in from the edge of body opening and into the head so terry cloth edge does not fray.

FISH-HEAD ALIEN

Enlarge template 160%.
Seam allowance is included.

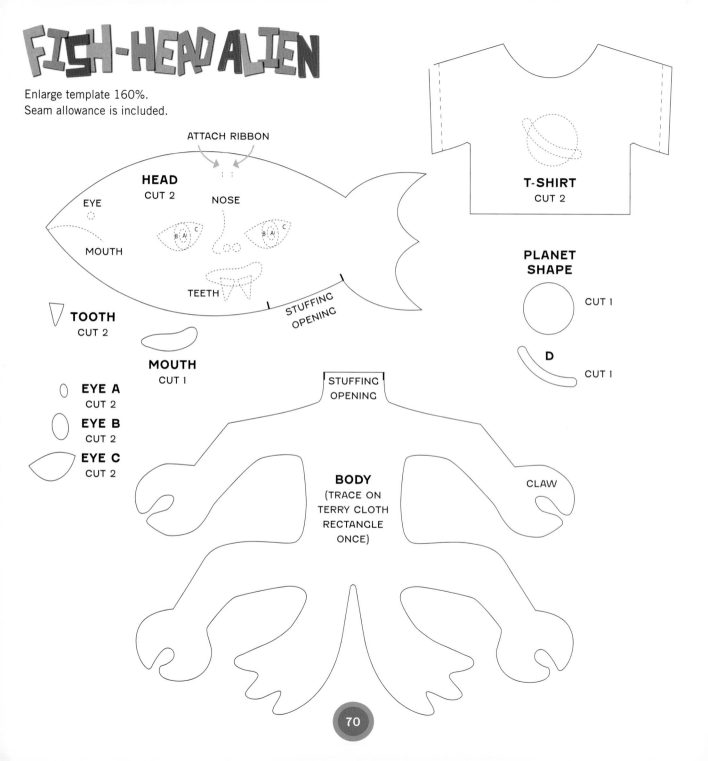

ATTACH RIBBON

HEAD
CUT 2

EYE

NOSE

MOUTH

B A C   B A C

TEETH

STUFFING
OPENING

TOOTH
CUT 2

MOUTH
CUT 1

EYE A
CUT 2

EYE B
CUT 2

EYE C
CUT 2

T-SHIRT
CUT 2

**PLANET
SHAPE**

CUT 1

D
CUT 1

STUFFING
OPENING

BODY
(TRACE ON
TERRY CLOTH
RECTANGLE
ONCE)

CLAW

KAPPA

This Japanese water deity is a prankster, so watch out for his gas passing and snack stealing. Children should offer crunchy cucumbers to this creature to avoid being his next meal. Also, be sure to note his special head pouch, which holds water and is key to his power. Try to spill the water to weaken him.

SKILL LEVEL

FINISHED SIZE: 7 inches wide by 7 inches high

Materials

FABRIC
- 4½ x 10 inches sea green velour
- 6½ x 13 inches upholstery remnant

FELT
- 1 sheet of yellow
- scrap of magenta

TRIM
- 2 white buttons
- yellow yarn for hair

FLOSS
- sea green, magenta

THREAD
- yellow

STUFFING

Preparation

CUT FROM PATTERNS:
- *From velour:* 2 head shapes, 1 base
- *From upholstery:* 2 body shapes
- *From yellow felt:* 1 mouth, 2 ear shapes, 2 leg shapes, 4 arm shapes
- *From magenta felt:* 2 head pouch shapes

CUT FREEHAND:
- *From yarn:* 1 strand 14 inches long, 16 strands 4 inches long
- *From magenta felt:* 2 circles the same size as the buttons

BEASTIE TIP Place your favorite trinket or a coin in your Kappa's head pouch. If he is pleased he will grant you a wish.

71

Instructions

1. Pin together body pieces, right sides facing in. Machine sew around but leave straight edge open along bottom. Align base with body, right sides facing in, and hand sew a whipstitch halfway around. Then turn body/base right side out.

2. Fill body with stuffing, tuck edges in, and sew opening closed with a whipstitch.

3. Embroider a swirl pattern on ears with sea green floss.

4. Take arms and legs and embroider lines (as marked on pattern) with sea green floss. Practice sewing on a scrap piece of felt the U-shape scales to see what size you like making. Embroider U-shaped scales on the front and back sides of arms and the front sides of legs. The embroidery will add extra sewing time so if you prefer to save time, skip step 4.

5. Pin two arm pieces together so right sides are facing out. Begin at point A and sew a running stitch with a double strand of yellow thread all the way around and stop at B. Then align arm on body. Arm should split open so one side is to the front and the other side is to the back of the body. Then continue a ladder stitch through body to attach arm on front and back sides. Repeat with other arm pieces.

6. Pin legs onto the front side of body. Sew a running stitch around the curve of the legs to attach to body.

7. With a double strand of magenta floss, embroider a frown line and nostrils on mouth piece. Next, place mouth piece on right side of head and sew to attach. This will be the front side of the head.

8. Place front head piece, right side up, on your work surface. Place the ears (X to X) pointing in toward the head. Then place second head piece, right side facing down, on top. Machine sew around head, leaving top open (between C and D), for turning right side out and stuffing.

9. Turn head right side out. Place magenta felt circles on front side of head. Then place buttons slightly lower down, so felt color shows past them, and sew four times through to attach button and felt to head.

10. Create hair piece by folding longer yarn strand in half (so it is 7 inches long) and double knot at one end, leaving an inch of slack. Then take the sixteen small strands and tie each onto strand with a double knot. Yarn should be evenly spaced apart. Align hair piece to top edge of head opening. Begin at the center of the back side and sew a whipstitch around to attach yarn along head edge.

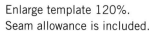

11. Fill head with a small amount of stuffing so it is squishy. Sew head pouch pieces together with a whipstitch along curved edge. Then place head pouch into head partway, leaving about ¼ inch of felt sticking out. Fold felt over to cover head edge. Sew a whipstitch around the head area (C to D) on front and back to attach pouch. Trim hair as you like.

12. Place head on top of body and sew a ladder stitch along the top, near the seam of body, to attach.

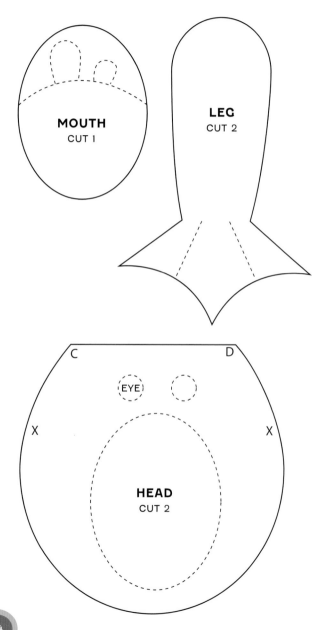

MOUTH
CUT 1

LEG
CUT 2

C   D

EYE

X   X

HEAD
CUT 2

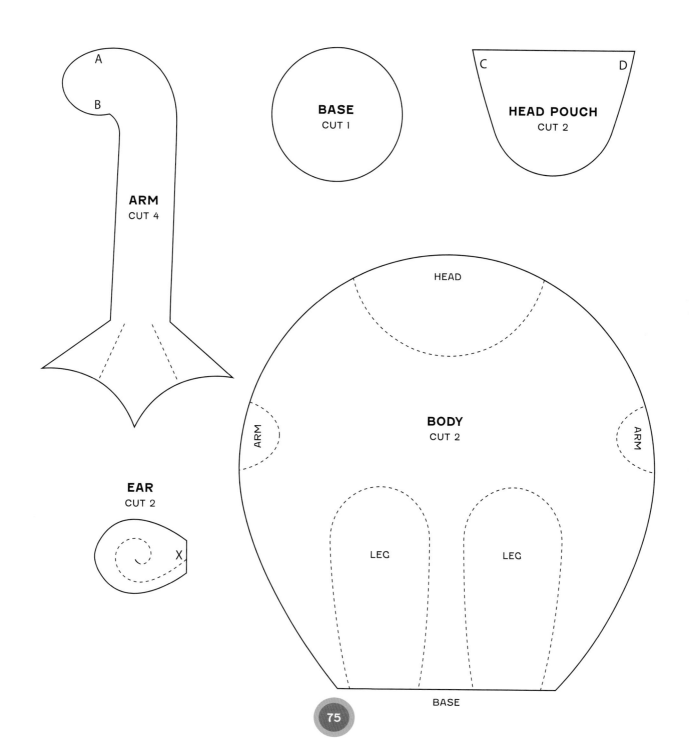

ARM
CUT 4

A

B

BASE
CUT 1

HEAD POUCH
CUT 2

C

D

EAR
CUT 2

X

HEAD

ARM

ARM

BODY
CUT 2

LEG

LEG

BASE

MINATA-KARAIA

In Brazil be careful when picking what appears to be a ripe coconut from a tree because you may actually be pulling fruit from the armpits of the Minata-Karaia. These tree giants grow their own food and they crack it open against their head. Listen and you can also hear a melody whistling from the hole in their head.

SKILL LEVEL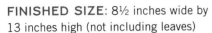

FINISHED SIZE: 8½ inches wide by 13 inches high (not including leaves)

Materials

FABRIC
• 9½ x 25 inch green cotton print

FELT
• 1 sheet of emerald green
• scrap of sage green

TRIM
• 8 brown pom-poms (medium and/or light brown)

FLOSS
• cinnamon red

THREAD
• dark green

STUFFING

CRAFT GLUE

Preparation

CUT FROM PATTERNS:
• *From cotton print:* 2 left arm shapes (cut 1 in reverse), 2 right arm shapes (cut 1 in reverse), 2 leg shapes
• *From emerald green felt:* 2 body shapes with holes cut out
• *From sage green felt:* 1 mouth, 2 leaves, 2 eyes

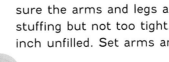

BEASTIE TIP The Minata-Karaia loves to be entertained by music. Play a tune and he might dance.

Instructions

1. Pin together left arm pieces, right arm pieces, and leg pieces, right sides facing in. Machine sew each pairing together, leaving ends open for turning right side out and stuffing.

2. Carefully turn right side out. This can take a few minutes more than usual because the area is narrow and long. Then slowly fill arms and legs with stuffing. Add very small amounts at a time and push the stuffing all the way into the crevices. Make sure the arms and legs are filled evenly with stuffing but not too tight. Leave the top ½ inch unfilled. Set arms and legs aside.

MINATA-KARAIA

3. Pin body pieces together and sew a small whipstitch around the hole edges to close. Then place eyes on the body. With three strands of floss sew two French knots through eyes. Place craft glue on the back of the mouth and attach to the body. Wait a few minutes for glue to set.

4. Place open ends of arms and legs between the two layers of felt (X to X) and (Y to Y), ½ inch deep, and pin in place. Begin sewing a topstitch at point A and continue around the body to B, leaving an area open for stuffing. Make sure arms and legs do not shift while sewing.

5. Leave the opening from A to B unsewn and fill the body with stuffing so it is squishy. Hand sew opening closed with a backstitch.

6. One at a time, sew thread through center of pom-poms and stitch each into the seam of the "armpit" area to attach.

7. Cut both leaves so they appear fringed. Attach each leaf (L to L) to the left and right corner of the body at the top, sewing three stitches through each leaf.

CUSTOMIZE YOUR BEASTIE

Make up a new Beastie but use the same pattern. Give him a new name and location. Change the color combination to reds, oranges, or blues. For example, your Beastie could have orange fruit that he squeezes against his head to make juice. Use orange pom-poms and a more citrus-colored fabric and felt.

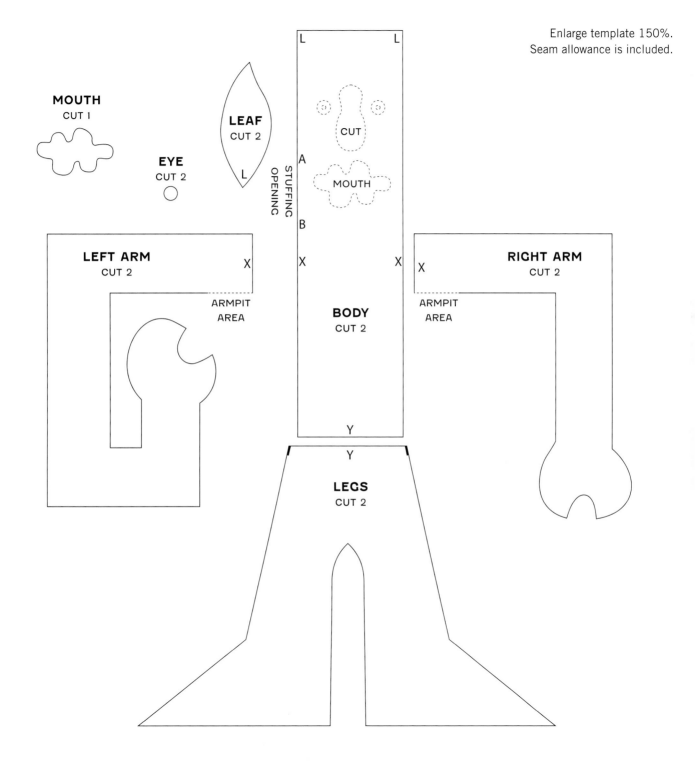

MOUTH
CUT 1

LEAF
CUT 2

EYE
CUT 2

L L

STUFFING OPENING

A

CUT

MOUTH

B

X X X X

LEFT ARM
CUT 2

RIGHT ARM
CUT 2

ARMPIT
AREA

ARMPIT
AREA

BODY
CUT 2

Y
Y

LEGS
CUT 2

L

Enlarge template 150%.
Seam allowance is included.

The loch can be a lonely place for a scaly sea monster in Scotland. Nessie hopes one day to find a buddy to keep him company in the murky waters. Occasionally he swims to the surface and takes a peek to see what's new. However, he never stays too long because he is afraid of the humans who aim their flashing boxes at him.

SKILL LEVEL

FINISHED SIZE: 9 ½ inches wide by 5 inches high

Materials

FABRIC
- 9 x 18 inch snakeskin vinyl or snakeskin cotton print
- 1¾ x 4½ inch wool or fleece

TRIM
- 2 metal buttons
- frayed fabric scrap (sometimes fabric or upholstery has a rough edge and can be trimmed and used as fray, or yarn can also be used—take a few pieces and make a tight knot at one end and trim so it is about 1¼ inches long)
- 4 pieces of small black rickrack 7 inches long

THREAD
- black, light green or other light color

STUFFING

Preparation

CUT FROM PATTERNS:
- *From vinyl:* 2 body shapes (cut 1 in reverse), 8 flipper shapes (cut 4 in reverse)
- *From wool or fleece:* 1 base

Note: Vinyl can rip easily so I prefer to hand sew it. Also be gentle when turning fabric right side out. If you decide to use another material, such as cotton, you can machine sew instead but Nessie will be slightly smaller.

BEASTIE TIP Nessie is known to have an insatiable appetite for haggis. Leave a plate aside and he may come up for a bite.

Instructions

1. Pin together body pieces, right sides facing in. Hand sew around the body, using a small whipstitch. Leave the section between A and B open. Next, pin base to body (A to A and B to B), right sides facing in. Beginning at A, sew along one side with a whipstitch until point B. Leave the rest unsewn for turning right side out and stuffing.

2. Turn right side out and stuff, making sure to fill head and neck first and then continue with the rest of the body. Sew opening closed with a small whipstitch.

NESSIE

3. Place fray where eye will be and sew a few stitches to attach. With green thread sew button eyes over the area where fray is stitched.

4. For each left flipper, pin together two flipper pieces, right sides facing in, and sew with whipstitch. Repeat for the two right flippers. Leave ends open for turning right side out and stuffing.

5. Turn all four flippers right side out and fill with stuffing. Close openings with a small whipstitch.

6. Sew one length of rickrack to each flipper along the seam. Begin at one end and sew in and out of rickrack edges and into seam. Continue sewing all the way around the flipper edge and trim off any extra rickrack at the end.

7. Place flippers as marked in pattern on the body, with ends pointing toward the tail. Hand sew flippers using a ladder stitch to attach.

Enlarge template 140%.
Seam allowance is included.

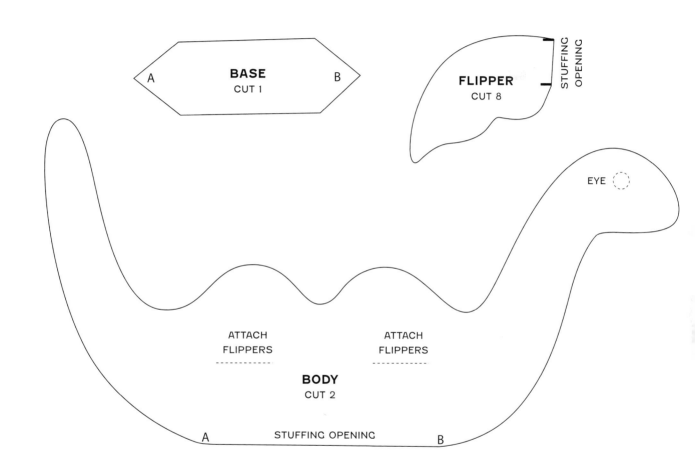

BASE
CUT 1

A

B

FLIPPER
CUT 8

STUFFING
OPENING

EYE

ATTACH
FLIPPERS

ATTACH
FLIPPERS

BODY
CUT 2

A

STUFFING OPENING

B

SIREN

The Siren, half female, half bird, evokes great beauty through sight and sound. However, she has looks to kill, and the song she sings is deadly, hypnotizing sailors so they navigate their vessel into the rocks, causing a shipwreck. These flightless, featherless creatures are stuck on an island off Italy for eternity.

SKILL LEVEL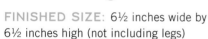

FINISHED SIZE: 6½ inches wide by 6½ inches high (not including legs)

Materials

FABRIC
- 7 x 9 inch colorful cotton print
- 8 x 9 inch iridescent orange

FELT
- scrap of magenta
- scrap of yellow

TRIM
- 2 turquoise beads

THREAD
- orange, yellow, turquoise

STUFFING

CRAFT GLUE

Preparation

CUT FROM PATTERNS:
- *From cotton print:* 2 body shapes (cut 1 in reverse)
- *From iridescent orange:* 4 wing shapes (cut 2 in reverse), 2 head shapes (cut 1 in reverse)
- *From magenta felt:* 2 hair pieces, 1 mouth
- *From yellow felt:* 4 leg shapes, 1 nose

BEASTIE TIP Remember to bring earplugs when sailing on the open waters to be safe from the call of the Siren.

Instructions

1. Pin a head piece to a body piece so right sides are facing in. Machine sew to attach head to body. Repeat with the other head and body pieces.

2. Next, place one head/body piece, right side facing up, on your work surface and place the other head/body piece on top, right side facing down. Pin and sew together, leaving an area unsewn for turning right side out and stuffing.

3. Turn head/body right side out. Use small amounts of stuffing to fill the head first and then continue filling the body until the Siren is evenly filled. Sew opening closed with a whipstitch.

4. Align both hair pieces and sew a whipstitch along the top from A to B. Place a small amount of stuffing inside the top area that rests on the Siren's head. (This will give the hair piece some height so it sits raised on the head.) Place hair piece on top of head. Make two stitches each at points A and C, sewing from underneath and into head.

5. Sew a bead eye onto each side of the head. Use at least four stitches so the beads are firmly in place. Next, sew a few stitches to attach the nose to the head. Then cut a tiny slit in the mouth to separate lips. Use a small dab of craft glue on the back and place the mouth on the head. Allow glue to set.

6. Take two wing pieces and pin them together so right sides are facing out. Sew a whipstitch with a double strand of turquoise thread all the way around the wings on the right side of fabric. Repeat with the other two wing pieces. The wings will have a slightly rough edge.

7. Align wings to body and sew from D to E to attach.

8. Pin together two leg pieces and sew a whipstitch around the entire edge. Repeat with the other two leg pieces. Place one leg on either side of the body (F to F) and sew a few stitches to attach.

CUSTOMIZE YOUR BEASTIE
For the Siren's body, try a cotton fabric with an "island" style, such as seashells, palm leaves, or tropical flowers.

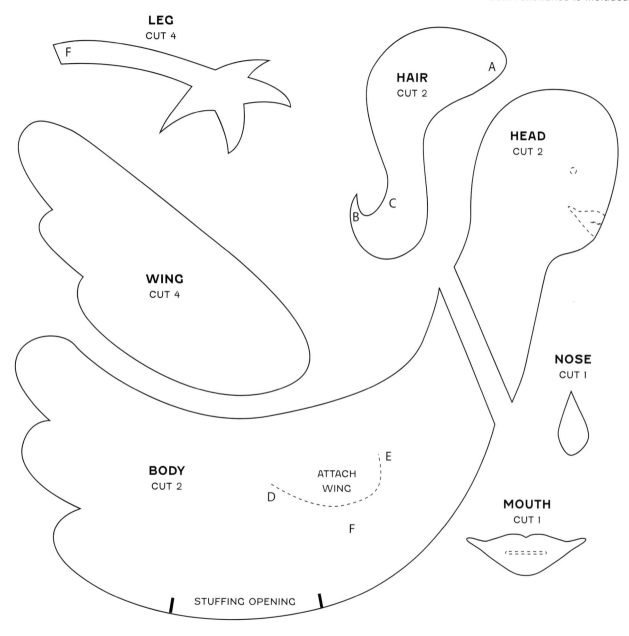

LEG
CUT 4

F

HAIR
CUT 2

A

HEAD
CUT 2

C

B

WING
CUT 4

NOSE
CUT 1

BODY
CUT 2

**ATTACH
WING**

E

D

F

MOUTH
CUT 1

STUFFING OPENING

TOMTE

In Sweden this creature watches over the farmhouse at night and tidies up any leftover messes. He protects and brings good luck to the family who dwells there. In order to keep a Tomte happy, make sure there is a toasty fire and a bowl of warm porridge and butter waiting for him. An unhappy Tomte will become red in the face, make a mess of the farm, and tie your horses' tails together.

SKILL LEVEL

FINISHED SIZE: 5½ inches wide by 6½ inches high (including hands)

Materials

FABRIC
- 5½ x 5 inch red-and-gray-striped cotton knit
- scrap of white faux fur, felt, or fleece

FELT
- 1 sheet of gray
- 1 sheet of blue
- scrap of yellow

TRIM
- 1 pom-pom

FLOSS
- navy blue

THREAD
- red, gray

STUFFING

Preparation

CUT FROM PATTERNS:
- *From cotton knit:* 2 hat shapes (use Baba Yaga's hat pattern)
- *From gray felt:* 2 body shapes (use Baba Yaga's head pattern), 2 hand shapes
- *From blue felt:* 2 shoe shapes
- *From yellow felt:* 2 shoe shapes (you will notice that the yellow shoes are slightly larger than the blue)
- *From faux fur:* 1 beard

CUT FREEHAND:
- *From blue felt:* 1 rectangular piece 1½ x 8½ inches for vest

BEASTIE TIP Hide your butter from a Tomte or he will eat it all.

Instructions

1. Pin hat pieces to body pieces, right sides facing in. Machine sew together.

2. Choose one of the hat/body pieces for the front. From the top measure ⅝ inch down the center of the body and mark a tiny dot for the nose. Measure ½ inch to the left and right of the dot, and mark tiny dots for where the eyes will be. Place pom-pom nose. Sew from the back side of the felt and through the back of the pom-pom, making two or three stitches to attach. Next, take three strands of embroidery floss and sew a French knot for each eye.

3. Place front hat/body piece, right side facing up, on your work surface. Place hands 1¼ inches down from the hat/body seam, along the sides. Hands should be pointing in toward the body with the thumbs facing down. Place the other hat/body piece, right side facing down, on top and pin. Begin from right corner and machine sew around, leaving a 2-inch opening on the bottom to turn right side out and to stuff.

4. Turn hat/body right side out and fill with stuffing. Sew a small whipstitch to close the opening.

5. On the blue shoes sew laces with red thread by making four cross stitches. Place yellow shoes behind the blue ones and sew a whipstitch around to attach shoes together, leaving a small gap. Put a pinch of stuffing into shoes, sew them shut, and place shoes along the bottom seam 1½ inches in from the corners. Sew a small running stitch to attach.

6. Cut armholes in the felt vest rectangle: Measure 2 inches in from one end and make a fold as shown in the diagram. Cut a tiny half oval at the center of the fold. Unfold felt and you should have a small oval hole cut out. Repeat on other side. Gently bring the Tomte's hands through armholes so the vest opening is in the front.

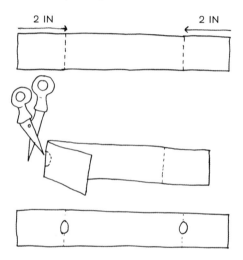

7. Place beard on head so eyes and nose go through opening. Sew two stitches at each corner to secure the beard.

CUSTOMIZE YOUR BEASTIE

Use a different color pom-pom for the nose. A yellow nose is for a Tomte who loves butter, a blue nose is for a Tomte who likes blueberries, and a red nose is for one who likes cherries.

Template shown at 100%.
Seam allowance is included.

NOTE:
CUT 2 HAT PIECES (USE BABA YAGA'S HAT PATTERN)
CUT 2 BODY PIECES (USE BABA YAGA'S HEAD PATTERN)

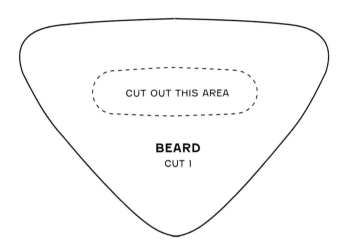

CUT OUT THIS AREA

BEARD
CUT 1

HAND
CUT 2

BLUE SHOE
CUT 2

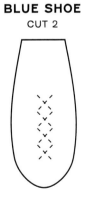

YELLOW SHOE
CUT 2

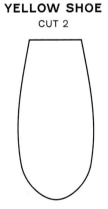

WEREWOLF

Have you ever wondered about your crazy neighbor with the unibrow, long fingernails, and a swinging stride? By day he just seems peculiar, but at night he's a hungry Werewolf. During a full moon the Werewolf curse takes over the stricken human and turns him into a hairy beast.

SKILL LEVEL

FINISHED SIZE: 16 inches wide by 16 inches high (depending on length of faux fur hair)

Materials

FABRIC
- 18 x 24 inch multicolored faux fur

FELT
- 3 sheets of blue
- scrap of white

TRIM
- 2 large metal beads

THREAD
- blue

STUFFING

Preparation

CUT FROM PATTERNS:
- *From faux fur:* 2 body shapes (cut 1 in reverse), 2 tail shapes (cut 1 in reverse), 4 limb shapes (cut 2 in reverse), 1 jaw shape
- *From blue felt:* 4 limb shapes, 1 jaw shape, 8 paw shapes, 2 ears, 1 nose (use ear pattern but cut out on inside line to make a nostril hole)
- *From white felt:* 4 claws, 4 teeth

CUT FREEHAND:
- *From blue felt:* 1 piece 2¼ x 12 inches for belly

BEASTIE TIP To stay safe from a Werewolf while taking an evening stroll, wear silver jewelry.

Instructions

1. Pin together body pieces so right sides are facing in and machine sew from A to B (around head and down back). Place teeth on one side pointing in toward the head (T to T). Then pin belly along C–D–E on one side so felt is facing in toward the right (furry) side of fur. Sew along C–D–E. Repeat and place teeth on other side, pin belly piece, and sew along C–D–E. Leave the area from A to E on head unsewn. Turn body right side out through opening B–C.

2. Fold ears in half lengthwise (X to X). Machine sew along X to Y. Place ears on head with the open side facing toward the back of the Werewolf. Sew three stitches at X and three at Y to secure ears to head. Next, sew bead eyes onto head. Use more stitches if the beads are heavy, and fewer if they're lightweight. For my Werewolf, I sewed four stitches, one on the left, top, right, and bottom of the bead, to secure it because it was heavy.

WEREWOLF

3. Next, pinch felt at open end of head (A–E) so corners meet and sew opening closed. Fold nose piece in half (X to X). Machine or hand sew nose closed along X to Z. Turn nose inside out. Place the pointed side of the nose so it faces away from the Werewolf's head, with the nostril hole facing down. Pinch faux fur at A–E on head and place into nose opening X–Y about ⅜ inches deep. Hand sew through faux fur to attach to side X–Y.

4. Take four paw pieces and two claws and make two hand paws: Place one claw on curved side of one paw piece as shown in diagram 1. Place second paw piece on top, pin, and sew a topstitch around felt to attach pieces together. Repeat for second hand paw. With remaining four paws and two claws make two foot paws: Place claw along longer straight side as shown in diagram 2. Place other paw piece on top, pin, and sew a topstitch along felt to attach pieces together. Repeat for second foot paw.

DIAGRAM 1

HAND PAW

DIAGRAM 2

FOOT PAW

5. To make the arm and leg limbs pin each faux fur limb piece, right side facing in, to a felt limb piece and sew together. Leave area open on side where paw attaches. Turn limbs right side out. Attach hand paws to arms and feet paws to legs by sewing with whipstitch. See diagram 3.

DIAGRAM 3

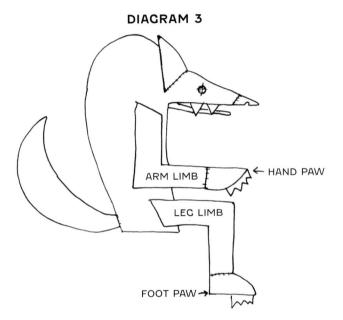

ARM LIMB

← HAND PAW

LEG LIMB

FOOT PAW →

6. Place arm and leg limbs on body (L to L) and sew with ladder stitch to attach, sewing from the inside.

7. Pin felt jaw piece to faux fur piece, right sides facing in. Machine sew jaw together, leaving area D–D open, and turn right side out. Do not stuff jaw. Sew opening closed with a whipstitch. Place jaw so felt side is facing up. Attach jaw to body (D–D to D–D) by sewing with ladder stitch.

8. Fill head and body with stuffing. Pinch corners (C to C) so they meet, and sew together with three stitches. Sew opening B–C closed with a whipstitch.

9. Pin the tail pieces together so right sides are facing in. Sew the tail together, leaving an opening for turning right side out and stuffing.

10. Turn tail right side out and fill with stuffing. Sew opening closed with a whipstitch.

11. Sew a ladder stitch to attach tail to body. Make sure stitches are tight and secure.

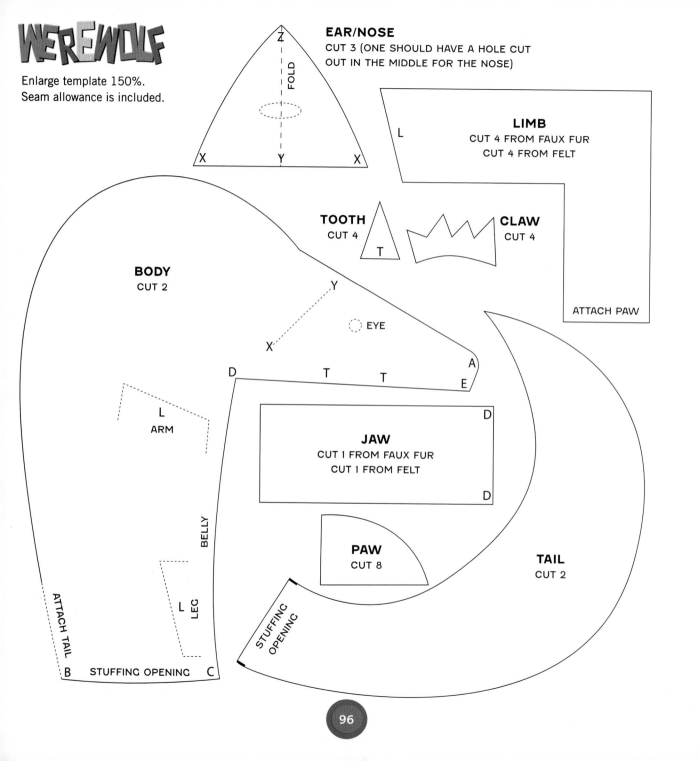

WEREWOLF

Enlarge template 150%.
Seam allowance is included.

EAR/NOSE
CUT 3 (ONE SHOULD HAVE A HOLE CUT
OUT IN THE MIDDLE FOR THE NOSE)

Z
FOLD
X Y X

LIMB
CUT 4 FROM FAUX FUR
CUT 4 FROM FELT
L

ATTACH PAW

TOOTH
CUT 4
T

CLAW
CUT 4

BODY
CUT 2

Y

EYE

X

A
D T T E

JAW
CUT 1 FROM FAUX FUR
CUT 1 FROM FELT
D

D

L
ARM

BELLY

PAW
CUT 8

TAIL
CUT 2

L LEG

ATTACH TAIL

STUFFING OPENING

STUFFING OPENING

B STUFFING OPENING C

The Yeti is the legendary guardian of the frostbitten mountain peaks of the Himalayas. He is usually in hiding but you can spot his remarkable ice sculptures in the snow. If you are brave enough, try placing some peanut butter cup ice cream just far enough away to lure a Yeti out. Have your camera ready.

SKILL LEVEL

FINISHED SIZE: 14 inches wide by 21 inches high

Materials

FABRIC
• 12 x 21 inch faux fur (white mixture or plain white)
• 7½ x 18 inch blue fleece or other soft fabric

FELT
• 1 sheet of magenta
• 1 sheet of white

TRIM
• 2 large shiny metallic beads

THREAD
• blue, brown, magenta

STUFFING

Preparation

CUT FROM PATTERNS:
• *From faux fur:* 2 body shapes, 2 full heads (then cut 1 of the heads along the dashed line into two pieces to make the top head piece and the chin piece), 8 paws
• *From fleece:* 4 arms (cut 2 in reverse), 4 legs
• *From magenta felt:* 1 mouth
• *From white felt:* 12 claws, 4 teeth

Note: The faux fur I used was too thick for my sewing machine so I hand sewed the fur. If you use fur with a shorter pile you can machine sew, but your Yeti will be slightly smaller than the dimensions given. When hand sewing through the thick faux fur I used a double strand of thread and a larger needle. One strand of sturdier coat or upholstery thread can also be used.

Instructions

1. Place two arm and two leg pieces, right sides facing up, on your work surface. Place remaining arm and leg pieces on top of these, right sides down. Machine sew along the sides. Turn arms and legs right side out.

2. Place four paw pieces, right sides facing up, on your work surface. Align three claws along the edge of each paw (C to C), with their points facing inward. Place remaining paw pieces on top, right sides facing down, and pin together. Make sure any fur sticking out is pushed inside the paw. Hand sew a whipstitch around the curved edge of paws. Turn paws right side out and set aside.

3. Place one body piece, right side facing up, on your work surface. Place arms on body (A–B to A–B) and legs on body (D–E to D–E), all pointing inward. Place second body piece on top, right side facing down. Now sew all the way around the body, leaving the top area, from A to A, open for turning right side out and stuffing. Sew carefully, making sure all layers are attached when sewing over areas from A to B and from D to E. You can leave arm and leg holes open but sew edge of faux fur side to fleece on front and back to connect.

4. Turn body right side out and set aside.

5. Make the front of the head: First place one tooth along upper mouth (T to T). Position mouth on top head piece (M–M to M–M). Sew a whipstitch on the wrong side of fabric to attach mouth to head along M–M. Next, place three teeth on the lower half of the mouth (T to T), pointing inward. Pin chin piece on lower mouth, right side facing down. Use a whipstitch to sew chin to mouth, making sure to sew through teeth. Once done, flip chin right side out.

6. Place full head piece, right side facing up, on your work surface. Place the front of the head (created in step 5), right side facing down, on top and sew together with a whipstitch. Leave area M–M unsewn for turning right side out and stuffing.

7. Turn head right side out. Arrange bead eyes on head and sew through bead holes eight to ten times, pulling thread tight to secure the large beads, and knot.

8. Fill body and head with stuffing. Attach head to body along area A–A. Sew a ladder stitch around tightly to attach.

9. Fill arms and legs evenly with stuffing. Pin paws to arms and legs (X to X). Sew a small ladder stitch or whipstitch around edge of each paw to attach to arm or leg.

CUSTOMIZE YOUR BEASTIE

Give your Yeti more bite by adding more teeth. Or make a Yeti family in different sizes by enlarging the pattern at various percentages on the copying machine. Use different-colored fleece fabrics for arms and legs.

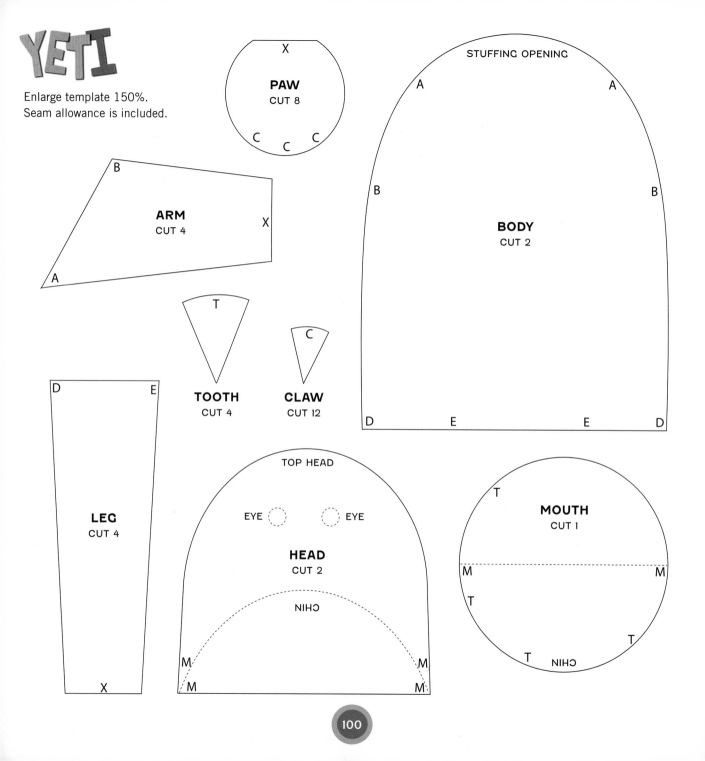

YETI

Enlarge template 150%.
Seam allowance is included.

PAW
CUT 8

X
C C C

BODY
CUT 2

STUFFING OPENING
A   A
B   B
D   E   E   D

ARM
CUT 4

B
X
A

TOOTH
CUT 4

T

CLAW
CUT 12

C

LEG
CUT 4

D   E
X

HEAD
CUT 2

TOP HEAD
EYE ◯   ◯ EYE
CHIN
M   M
M   M

MOUTH
CUT 1

T
M   M
T
T   T
T
CHIN

ZOMBIE

A sorcerer brings a corpse back to life as a soulless puppet—a Zombie—that he can control. Wait quietly in a cemetery in the dead of the night and you may see a Zombie creep out of the earth. Zombies do not speak and can be dangerous, so stay at a safe distance.

SKILL LEVEL

FINISHED SIZE: 3½ inches wide by 13 inches high

Materials

FABRIC
- 10 x 12 inch white cotton

FELT
- 1 sheet of black
- scrap of white
- scrap of red

TRIM
- 1 red pom-pom
- 1 gauze bandage (if you do not have a gauze bandage, try using bits of colorful frayed cloth)

THREAD
- black, white

STUFFING

CRAFT GLUE

Preparation

CUT FROM PATTERNS:
- *From cotton:* 2 body shapes (cut 1 in reverse)
- *From black felt:* 4 arm shapes, 4 foot shapes, 1 left ear, 1 right ear, 2 eyes A, 1 eye C
- *From white felt:* 1 eye B
- *From red felt:* 1 blood drop each A, B, and C; 2 blood drops D

CUT FREEHAND:
- *From black felt:* 1 small tooth ¼ x ¼ inch, 1 rectangle 1 x ¼ inch

BEASTIE TIP The foul stench the Zombie emits is strong, so hold your nose or you may pass out.

Instructions

1. Pin together two arm pieces for left arm and two pieces for right arm. Beginning at point A, sew a whipstitch around arm with white thread to attach both layers of felt. Sew clockwise about halfway around, stopping just past the hands at point B. If you are using fiberfill, take a small amount and knead it back and forth between your hands, as if it were clay, to make it thin and long. Then use a stuffing stick to push the stuffing into the arms carefully. The arms should be just filled so they are squishy. Continue sewing arms with a whipstitch, stopping at point C. Leave the opening from A to C unsewn. Set arms aside.

2. Align and pin two feet pieces together and sew using a whipstitch with white thread. Leave opening from D to E unsewn for stuffing opening. Repeat for second foot. Use a pinch of stuffing to fill feet. Sew opening of feet closed with a whipstitch.

3. Lay one body piece, right side up, on your work surface. Place left and right ear on top, pointing inward. Pin in place. Place second body piece, right side facing down, on top and pin in place. Machine sew body, leaving an area open for turning right side out and stuffing.

4. Turn body right side out and fill with stuffing. Sew the opening closed with a small whipstitch.

5. Sew a whipstitch to attach straight edge of feet to the bottom edge of legs at point X.

6. Next, attach both arms. Align arms perpendicular to body (C–A to C–A) and allow unsewn area of felt to spread out to front and back of body. Sew a tight whipstitch to attach.

7. Put glue on back of one eye A and place on eye B. Then glue back of eye B to eye C. Glue completed eye to face. Allow glue to set for a few minutes. Glue the other black eye A to the center of the pom-pom. Sew one end of the black rectangle to the other end to form a loop. Sew three stitches through the pom-pom to attach it to the loop. Sew three stitches on the opposite side of the loop to attach to the face. Next, use a double strand of thread to embroider a mouth. Use a small amount of glue to attach the tooth. Finally sew a few strands of thread through the top to make hair stick out of the Zombie's head.

8. Glue blood drops to front and back of the Zombie's body.

9. Cut and fray gauze pieces and place on arms and the front and back of the Zombie's body. Attach with a tiny bit of glue.

CUSTOMIZE YOUR BEASTIE
Try reversing the colors of the Zombie's body and arms. Substitute black for white and vice versa.

ZOMBIE

Enlarge template 140%.
Seam allowance is included.

E   X   D

FOOT
CUT 4

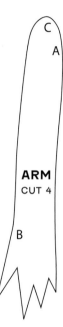

C

A

ARM
CUT 4

B

EYE A
CUT 2

EYE B
CUT 1

EYE C
CUT 1

LEFT EAR
CUT 1

RIGHT EAR
CUT 1

**BLOOD
DROP A**
CUT 1

**BLOOD
DROP B**
CUT 1

**BLOOD
DROP C**
CUT 1

**BLOOD
DROP D**
CUT 2

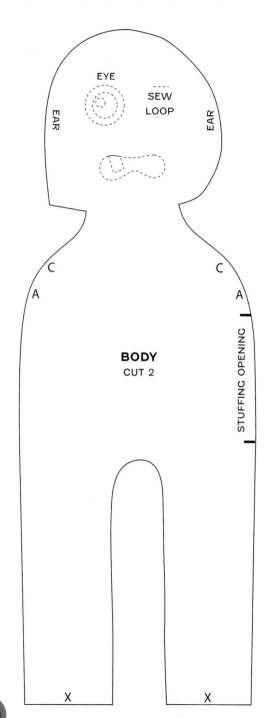

EYE

SEW
LOOP

EAR

EAR

C

A

C

A

BODY
CUT 2

STUFFING OPENING

X

X

INDEX